The Delia Collection
Italian

BBC BOOKS

Published by BBC Books
BBC Worldwide Ltd
Woodlands
80 Wood Lane
London W12 OTT

First published in 2004

Edited for BBC Worldwide Ltd
by New Crane Ltd

Editor: Sarah Randell
Designer: Paul Webster
Sub-editors: Heather Cupit, Diana Galligan
Picture Editor: Diana Hughes
Recipe Testing: Pauline Curran
and the New Crane Food Team
Commissioning Editor for the BBC: Vivien Bowler

ISBN 0 563 48735 6

Printed and bound in Italy
by L.E.G.O SpA
Colour separation by Radstock Reproductions Ltd
Midsomer Norton

Cover and title page photographs: Peter Knab and Michael Paul
For further photographic credits, see page 136

Introduction

When I look back over my years of cookery writing, I have to admit that very often, decisions about what to do have sprung from what my own particular needs are. As a very busy person who has to work, run a home and cook, I felt it was extremely useful to have, for instance, summer recipes in one book – likewise winter and Christmas, giving easy access to those specific seasons.

This, my latest venture, has come about for similar reasons. Thirty four years of recipe writing have produced literally thousands of recipes. So I now feel what would be really helpful is to create a kind of ordered library (so I don't have to rack my brains and wonder which book this or that recipe is in!). Thus, if I want to make an Italian recipe, I don't have to look through the Italian sections of various books, but have the whole lot in one convenient collection.

In compiling these books, I have chosen what I think are the best and most popular recipes and, at the same time, have added some that are completely new. It is my hope that those who have not previously tried my recipes will now have smaller collections to sample, and that those dedicated followers will appreciate an ordered library to provide easy access and a reminder of what has gone before and may have been forgotten.

This Italian book is a collection of recipes I have acquired over the years. Since spending the summer working in Italy when I was 21, I have been an enthusiastic devotee of Italian cookery always returning from holidays with ideas and trying to emulate them. So I would like to emphasise that the recipes in this collection are very much my own interpretation of this greatly loved cuisine.

Delia Smith

Conversion Tables

All these are approximate conversions, which have either been rounded up or down. In a few recipes it has been necessary to modify them very slightly. Never mix metric and imperial measures in one recipe, stick to one system or the other.

All spoon measurements used throughout this book are level unless specified otherwise.

All butter is salted unless specified otherwise.

All recipes have been double-tested, using a standard convection oven. If you are using a fan oven, adjust the cooking temperature according to the manufacturer's handbook.

Weights

½ oz	10 g
¾	20
1	25
1½	40
2	50
2½	60
3	75
4	110
4½	125
5	150
6	175
7	200
8	225
9	250
10	275
12	350
1 lb	450
1 lb 8 oz	700
2	900
3	1.35 kg

Volume

2 fl oz	55 ml
3	75
5 (¼ pint)	150
10 (½ pint)	275
1 pint	570
1¼	725
1¾	1 litre
2	1.2
2½	1.5
4	2.25

Dimensions

⅛ inch	3 mm
¼	5
½	1 cm
¾	2
1	2.5
1¼	3
1½	4
1¾	4.5
2	5
2½	6
3	7.5
3½	9
4	10
5	13
5¼	13.5
6	15
6½	16
7	18
7½	19
8	20
9	23
9½	24
10	25.5
11	28
12	30

Oven temperatures

Gas mark 1	275°F	140°C
2	300	150
3	325	170
4	350	180
5	375	190
6	400	200
7	425	220
8	450	230
9	475	240

Contents

Antipasti

Giardiniera
(Italian garden pickles)

4 oz (110 g) red onions

4 oz (110 g) courgettes

6 oz (175 g) aubergine

4½ oz (125 g) trimmed fennel bulb

½ medium red pepper

½ medium yellow pepper

2 oz (50 g) button mushrooms

3 oz (75 g) sea salt

3 cloves garlic, thinly sliced

2 oz (50 g) cherry tomatoes
or small vine tomatoes

3½ tablespoons olive oil

17 fl oz (480 ml)
good-quality white wine vinegar

4 fresh bay leaves

4 small sprigs each fresh rosemary
and thyme

8 black peppercorns

You will also need two 17½ fl oz
(500 ml) preserving jars, sterilised
(see recipe method).

I had a spell of work in Italy when I was 21, and one of my abiding memories of all those Italian meals was that Sunday lunch always began with a plate of salamis, prosciutto and mortadella served with pickled vegetables. I loved the way the pickles cut through the richness of the meats. This recipe comes from chef Lucy Crabb.

This has to begin the night before with the normal salting process. Work your way through the list of vegetables until they are all prepared: cut the onion into 8 wedges through the root; next, cut the courgettes and aubergine into thick matchsticks, and the fennel bulb into wedges; lastly, core and deseed the peppers and cut them into 2 inch (5 cm) chunks. Now layer all the vegetables, including the mushrooms, but not the garlic and tomatoes, in a non-metallic bowl and, as you pile them in, sprinkle salt between the layers. Now pour over 1½ pints (850 ml) of water, cover with a plate with a weight on it to submerge the vegetables, and leave the bowl in a cool place overnight.

Next day, drain the vegetables in a colander, then rinse them well under cold, running water. Now shake off the excess water, dry them in a clean tea cloth, and leave them spread out for about 3 hours on another clean tea cloth to dry off thoroughly. After that, tip the vegetables into a bowl and stir in the garlic, along with the tomatoes and olive oil.

Now sterilise the jars. To do this, wash the jars and lids in warm, soapy water, rinse well (again in warm water), then dry them thoroughly with a clean tea cloth, place them on a baking tray and pop them in a medium oven, gas mark 4, 350°F (180°C) for a minimum of 5 minutes.

Next, pour a thin layer of vinegar into the bottom of the hot, sterilised jars and add a bay leaf, a sprig of rosemary and a sprig of thyme. Then pack in the vegetables, adding the remainder of the herbs and the peppercorns as you go, and pour in enough vinegar over each layer to ensure the vegetables are covered completely. Now swivel the jars to make sure the air is expelled and really press the vegetables down under the liquid before you cover with vinegar-proof (non-metallic) lids. Label when cold and store the pickles in a cool, dry, dark place to mellow for a month before eating. They will keep for up to 3 months, but the vibrant colour will fade slightly.

Antipasti

Parma Ham with Figs

Parma ham – *prosciutto di Parma* – is from the Emilia-Romagna region of Italy and is wonderful served with fresh juicy figs (or wedges of ripe melon) as a first course. Arrange thinly sliced Parma ham on serving plates. Cut some ripe figs in half or quarters, depending on their size, and serve them with the Parma ham, drizzled with a little olive oil and seasoned with freshly milled black pepper.

Assorted Meats and Mozzarella

This is one of my favourite Italian first courses. If you can buy the meats and cheese from a specialist Italian deli, so much the better. All you need to do is divide slices of mortadella, Parma ham, salami and some sliced mozzarella equally among serving plates. Then garnish with olives, cornichons and radishes or some sharp Giardiniera, Italian garden pickles (see page 8). Just before serving, drizzle the mozzarella with some olive oil and season with freshly milled black pepper. Then all you need is some warm Italian bread and good creamy butter.

Parmesan (Parmigiano Reggiano) with Pears

Parmesan deserves to be enjoyed just as it is, as a nibble with apéritifs before a meal. Best of all, use a traditional, almond-shaped Parmesan knife that is used to crumble the cheese rather than cut the pieces off it (so leaving the texture intact), and serve it with ripe pears and a dry, light Lambrusco.

Roasted Figs with Gorgonzola and Honey-vinegar Sauce

This may sound like an unlikely combination but it's a simply brilliant first course. All you do is wipe and halve some figs, then place them, cut side up, on a baking tray. Season with salt and freshly milled black pepper, then pop them under a pre-heated grill for 5-6 minutes, until they're soft and just bubbling slightly. Then, crumble some Gorgonzola Piccante on to each one, gently pressing it down to squash it in a bit. Then pop the figs back under the grill for about 2 minutes, until the cheese is bubbling and faintly golden brown. Meanwhile, make a sauce by combining a couple of tablespoons each of runny honey and red wine vinegar, then serve the figs with the sauce poured over.

Piedmont Roasted Peppers
Serves 4

4 large, red peppers
(green are not suitable)

4 medium tomatoes

8 tinned anchovy fillets, drained

2 cloves garlic

8 dessertspoons extra virgin
olive oil

freshly milled black pepper

To serve

a small bunch of fresh basil leaves

You will also need a good,
solid, shallow roasting tray,
12 x 16 inches (30 x 40 cm), lightly
oiled. If the sides are too deep,
the roasted vegetables won't get
those lovely, nutty, toasted edges.

Pre-heat the oven to gas mark 4,
350°F (180°C).

This recipe is, quite simply, stunning: hard to imagine how something so easily prepared can taste so good. Its history is colourful, too. It was first discovered by Elizabeth David and published in her splendid book, *Italian Food*. Then the Italian chef Franco Taruschio at the Walnut Tree Inn, near Abergavenny, cooked it there. Simon Hopkinson, who ate it at the Walnut Tree, put it on his menu at his great London restaurant Bibendum, where I ate it – which is how it comes to be here now for you to make and enjoy.

Begin by cutting the peppers in half and removing the seeds, but leave the stalks intact (they're not edible, but they do look attractive and they help the pepper halves to keep their shape). Lay the pepper halves in the roasting tray. Now put the tomatoes in a bowl and pour boiling water over them. Leave the tomatoes for 1 minute, then drain them and slip the skins off (using a cloth to protect your hands). Then cut the tomatoes into quarters and place 2 quarters in each pepper half.

After that, snip 1 anchovy fillet per pepper half into rough pieces and add to the tomatoes. Peel the garlic cloves, slice them thinly and divide the slices equally among the tomatoes and anchovies. Now spoon 1 dessertspoon of the olive oil into each pepper half, season with freshly milled pepper (but no salt because of the anchovies) and place the tray on a high shelf in the oven for the peppers to roast for 50 minutes to 1 hour. Then transfer the cooked peppers to a serving dish, with all the precious juices poured over, and garnish with a few scattered basil leaves. These do need good bread to go with them, as the juices are sublime – focaccia would be perfect (see page 130).

Tomato, Mozzarella and Avocado Salad with Herb Vinaigrette
Serves 2

14 oz (400 g) ripe, red tomatoes

5 oz (150 g) baby mozzarella in brine (bocconcini)

1 medium avocado

¾ oz (20 g) fresh basil leaves

For the dressing

1 small clove garlic

1 teaspoon sea salt

1 teaspoon wholegrain mustard

1 dessertspoon white wine vinegar

3 tablespoons extra virgin olive oil

1 dessertspoon chopped fresh basil leaves

1 teaspoon chopped fresh tarragon

freshly milled black pepper

This one is a classic, known in Italy as *insalata tricolore*. It's not recorded if it was specifically created to echo the colours of the Italian flag, or whether some inspired chef assembled these ingredients and suddenly appreciated their significance. Either way, it's a lovely combination of textures and flavours. Mozzarella is now sold as baby bite-sized cheese called *bocconcini*, which look particularly attractive here.

Prepare the salad first. Thinly slice the tomatoes, then halve the avocado, remove and discard the stone and skin and thinly slice each half of the flesh. Drain the bocconcini and cut these in half (or if you're using a large mozzarella, cut it into thin slices). Now arrange the tomato and avocado slices on a serving plate in overlapping circles, starting from the edge, placing the whole basil leaves among the layers. Finally, place the mozzarella on top.

Make up the dressing by crushing the clove of garlic, together with the salt, in a pestle and mortar until it becomes a creamy mass. After that, add the mustard and work that into a paste, then add a good grinding of freshly milled black pepper, followed by the vinegar and lastly the oil, whisking everything until thoroughly amalgamated. Stir in the chopped herbs and, just before serving, drizzle the dressing over the salad.

Mozzarella in Carrozza
Serves 2

3 oz (75 g) mozzarella, thinly sliced

4 slices of white bread from a large loaf

2 slices Parma ham, if using

2 large eggs

2 tablespoons milk

1 tablespoon seasoned flour

vegetable oil for frying

salt

Literally 'mozzarella in a carriage' – the carriage being two slices of bread dipped in beaten egg and deep-fried. This makes a great snack and I've found the addition of a slice of Parma ham provides an interesting variation.

Prepare the first 'carriage' simply by placing half of the mozzarella (and a slice of Parma ham, if using) between 2 of the slices of bread (unbuttered). Then repeat with the rest of the bread and cheese (and ham). Next, lightly beat the eggs together with the milk, and pour the mixture into a shallow dish (to make coating easier). Spread the seasoned flour out on a largish plate – and now you're ready to go.

Pour about 1 inch (2.5 cm) of oil into a wide saucepan, or deep-sided frying pan, and heat it up to the point where a cube of bread thrown in turns golden brown in 1 minute. Then coat both sides of each sandwich with seasoned flour, and cut each of the sandwiches into 4 quarters. Dip each quarter into the beaten egg and milk to soak up the mixture on both sides. Now carefully slide the quarters into the hot oil. They will probably float on top of the oil, so cook them for 30 seconds on one side, then turn them over to cook for a further 30 seconds on the other side. When the coating is a nice golden brown, they're ready. Drain them on kitchen paper or crumpled greaseproof paper, sprinkle with salt and serve.

Grilled Polenta with Ham, Melted Fontina and Sage
Serves 6

easy-cook polenta, measured to the 4 fl oz (120 ml) level in a measuring jug

1 oz (25 g) Parmesan, finely grated

1 oz (25 g) softened butter

salt and freshly milled black pepper

For the topping

6 slices Parma ham

3 oz (75 g) fontina or Gruyère, cut into 6 slices

12 small fresh sage leaves

2 tablespoons olive oil

salt and freshly milled black pepper

You will also need a baking tin, 6 x 10 x 1 inches (15 x 25.5 x 2.5 cm), lined with baking parchment, a 3 inch (7.5 cm) pastry cutter, and a small baking tray, lightly oiled.

As well as being a brilliant starter, this can also be made into bite-sized canapés to serve with drinks.

First of all, make the polenta. To do this, pour 1 pint (570 ml) boiling water from the kettle into a large saucepan and allow it to come back to simmering point. Then add the polenta in a long, steady stream, along with half a teaspoon of salt, stirring all the time with a wooden spoon. Place the pan on a low heat and allow the polenta to cook for 5 minutes, continuing to stir, until thickened – it should look like yellow porridge.

As soon as the polenta is ready, season it generously with freshly milled black pepper, then stir in the Parmesan and butter. Taste to check the seasoning and add more salt and pepper, if necessary. Then, as quickly as you can, spoon the polenta into the lined baking tin, smooth the top with a palette knife and allow it to get quite cold.

When the polenta is cold, lift it out of the tin, cut it out into 6 circles with the cutter and place these on the baking tray. Next, pre-heat the grill to its highest setting for 10 minutes. Measure the olive oil into a saucer and brush each piece of polenta with some of it, then season generously again with salt and freshly milled black pepper. Now place the baking tray under the grill, about 4 inches (10 cm) below the heat source. Grill the polenta for 3 minutes on each side until it becomes golden and toasted at the edges, then remove it from the grill.

Next, loosely fold the pieces of ham and place 1 on top of each polenta round. Then arrange a slice of cheese on top of the ham and, finally, dip the sage leaves into the remaining olive oil and lay 2 on top of the cheese on each one. All this can be done in advance if you allow the grilled polenta to get cold before you put the topping on. When you are ready to serve the polenta, put them back under a hot grill for another 3-4 minutes, or until the cheese has melted and the sage leaves are crisp.

Bruschetta with Tomato and Basil
Serves 4-6 (makes 12)

1 ciabatta loaf, cut into
12 thin slices

1 clove garlic, rubbed in a little salt

about 6 tablespoons extra virgin
olive oil

For the topping

6 red, ripe, plum tomatoes

a few small fresh basil leaves

a few drops of extra virgin olive oil

sea salt and freshly milled
black pepper

Bruschetta is a very special type of toasted bread, pronounced 'brusketta'. When I first tasted the real thing in Tuscany, it was one of the most memorable eating experiences of my life. Italian country bread is toasted on both sides over hot, fragrant coals, then slashes are made along the surface of each piece of bread, which is then rubbed with an open clove of garlic. After that, peppery Italian extra virgin olive oil is poured over quite generously so that it runs into the bread, making little pools all around the base of the plate. The pleasure and joy in its utter simplicity are indescribable. Good bread, good olive oil – what more could you want? Just two things: very red, ripe plum tomatoes and basil leaves. It's perhaps the best bruschetta of all, and perfect with drinks before a meal instead of serving as a starter. Given that few of us have hot coals handy (though don't forget bruschetta during the barbecue season), the next best thing is a cast-iron, ridged griddle or, failing that, an ordinary domestic grill.

Prepare the tomatoes before toasting the bread. All you do is place them in a bowl, pour boiling water over them and leave for exactly 1 minute before draining the tomatoes and slipping off the skins (protect your hands with a cloth if they are too hot). Then chop the tomatoes finely.

Pre-heat the ridged griddle over a high heat for about 10 minutes. When it's really hot, place the slices of bread – on the diagonal – and grill them for about 1 minute on each side, until they're golden and crisp and have charred strips across each side. (Alternatively, toast them under a conventional grill.) Then, as they are ready, take a sharp knife and quickly make about 3 little slashes across each one, rub the garlic in and drizzle about half a tablespoon of olive oil over each slice.

When the bruschetta are made, top with the tomatoes and basil leaves, season with salt and freshly milled black pepper and sprinkle a few more drops of olive oil over before serving. It's hard to believe that something so simple can be so wonderful.

White Bean and Tuna Fish Salad with Lemon Pepper Dressing
Serves 6

9 oz (250 g) dried cannellini beans

14 oz (400 g) best-quality tuna in oil, in a tin or a jar

1 oz (25 g) rocket, stalks removed

2 oz (50 g) red onion, sliced into thin rounds

salt and freshly milled black pepper

For the dressing

grated zest of 1 lemon

3 tablespoons lemon juice

1 rounded teaspoon black peppercorns

2 cloves garlic

1 tablespoon sea salt

1 heaped teaspoon mustard powder

3 tablespoons extra virgin olive oil

This is my version of an old Italian favourite, and I think the addition of a sharp lemon dressing and some buttery rocket leaves gives a lovely edge. If you forget to soak the beans overnight, you can rinse them with cold water and place them in a saucepan, cover with plenty of water, bring up to the boil for 10 minutes, then turn off the heat and leave them to soak for 2 hours. Next, bring them up to the boil and simmer gently for $1\frac{1}{4}$-$1\frac{1}{2}$ hours, or until the beans are tender.

Ideally, begin this the night before you are going to make the salad by rinsing the beans, placing them in a bowl and covering them with cold water to soak. Next day, drain them, then put the beans in a large saucepan, cover with fresh water and bring them up to simmering point. Boil for 10 minutes, then cover and simmer gently for $1\frac{1}{4}$-$1\frac{1}{2}$ hours, or until tender.

Meanwhile, empty the tuna fish into a sieve fitted over a bowl and allow it to drain, reserving the oil. Then, to make the dressing, first crush the garlic and salt, using a pestle and mortar, till the garlic is pulverised, then work the mustard powder into this. Now push the mixture to one side, add the peppercorns and crush these fairly coarsely. Next, add the grated lemon zest, along with the lemon juice, olive oil and 3 tablespoons of the reserved tuna oil (the rest of the tuna oil can be discarded). Whisk everything together very thoroughly, then, when the beans are cooked, drain them, rinse out the saucepan and return the beans to it. Now pour the dressing over while the beans are still warm, give everything a good stir and season generously.

To serve the salad, arrange three-quarters of the rocket leaves over the base of a serving dish, spoon the beans on top and add the tuna fish in chunks. Then add the rest of the rocket leaves, pushing some of the leaves and chunks of tuna right in among the beans. Finally, arrange the onion slices on top and serve straightaway, allowing people to help themselves. Warm, crusty ciabatta bread would be an excellent accompaniment.

Minestrone with Rice
Serves 6

2 medium, ripe tomatoes

2 oz (50 g) smoked pancetta or streaky bacon, derinded and finely chopped

1 medium onion, finely chopped

2 celery stalks, trimmed and finely chopped

6 oz (175 g) carrots, finely chopped

1 clove garlic, crushed

8 oz (225 g) leeks

6 oz (175 g) green cabbage, finely shredded

carnaroli rice, measured to the 3 fl oz (75 ml) level in a measuring jug

1 oz (25 g) butter

1 tablespoon olive oil

2½ pints (1.5 litres) good chicken or vegetable stock

1 dessertspoon tomato purée

2 tablespoons chopped fresh parsley

1½ tablespoons chopped fresh basil

lots of freshly grated Parmesan, to serve

salt and freshly milled black pepper

Minestrone can be made in many variations with whatever is to hand. Sometimes I put small pasta in it, but this version has risotto rice, which absorbs all the flavour of the vegetables.

First of all, skin the tomatoes by putting them in a bowl and pouring boiling water over them. Leave the tomatoes for 1 minute exactly, then drain off the water and, as soon as they are cool enough to handle, slip off their skins and chop the tomatoes. Now heat the butter and oil in a large (6 pint/3.5 litre) saucepan, then add the pancetta or bacon and cook this for a minute or two before adding the onion, followed by the celery and carrots and then the tomatoes. Now stir in the crushed garlic and some salt and pepper, then cover and cook very gently for 20 minutes or so to allow the vegetables to sweat – give it an occasional stir to prevent the vegetables sticking.

Then pour in the stock and bring to the boil and then simmer gently, covered, for about 1 hour. To prepare the leeks, first take the tough green ends off and throw them out, then make a vertical split about halfway down the centre of each leek and clean them by running them under the cold water tap while you fan out the layers – this will rid them of any hidden dust and grit. Then finely chop them.

When the hour is up, stir the leeks, cabbage and rice into the stock and vegetables and cook, uncovered, for a further 10 minutes. Finally, stir in the tomato purée, cook for another 10 minutes and, just before serving, stir in the parsley and basil. Serve the minestrone in warmed soup bowls, sprinkled with Parmesan cheese.

Italian Stuffed Aubergines
Serves 6

3 medium aubergines

3-4 tablespoons olive oil

1 onion, chopped

1 large clove garlic, crushed

1 tablespoon chopped fresh basil, plus a few sprigs, to garnish

6 tinned anchovy fillets, drained and chopped

about 6 oz (175 g) mozzarella cheese, cut into thin slices

3 largish, ripe tomatoes, sliced

1½ tablespoons capers in vinegar, drained and chopped a little

salt and freshly milled black pepper

You will also need a small roasting tin or baking dish, lightly oiled.

This is a recipe I was served first of all in a restaurant in Amalfi many years ago. Luckily, I always have a notebook to hand, so this replication is, I think, every bit as good as the original.

Trim the green stalks from the aubergines and slice them in half lengthwise. Then, if you have a grapefruit knife use that, or otherwise a teaspoon, to get the pulpy centres out of the aubergines leaving a shell not less than ¼ inch (5 mm) thick. Sprinkle the shells liberally with salt and leave them upside down to drain for 45 minutes. Meanwhile, chop the pulp. Now heat 2 tablespoons of the oil in a saucepan and gently fry the onion until softened. Stir in the chopped pulp, crushed garlic and half the basil. Season with salt and pepper and cook over a low heat for about 10 minutes, stirring now and then. After this, stir in the chopped anchovies. Pre-heat the oven to gas mark 4, 350°F (180°C).

Next, wipe the aubergine shells with kitchen paper and arrange them in the roasting tin or baking dish. Spoon the onion mixture into the shells, then arrange alternate slices of cheese and tomato on top of each aubergine half and sprinkle with the chopped capers. Finally, sprinkle with the remaining basil and dribble a little more olive oil over each. Season and bake, uncovered, in the top of the oven for 40 minutes. Serve garnished with a sprig of fresh basil.

Pasta e Fagioli
Serves 4-6

4 oz (110 g) dried shortcut macaroni

8 oz (225 g) dried cannellini beans

2 tablespoons olive oil

1 large onion, finely chopped

2 cloves garlic, crushed

2½ tablespoons tomato purée

1 heaped tablespoon fresh rosemary, bruised in a mortar, then very finely chopped

Parmesan cheese, shaved or grated, to serve

salt and freshly milled black pepper

This is a big hefty Tuscan bean and pasta soup, perfect for the winter months, with a light main course. Alternatively, it is a complete lunch, with some cheese and a salad to follow.

Ideally, you need to start this soup the night before you want to make it by rinsing the dried cannellini beans in a sieve under cold water, and then soaking them in 3 pints (1.75 litres) of cold water overnight. If you are short of time, put the beans in a saucepan with the same amount of cold water, bring them up to the boil and give them about 10 minutes cooking before turning the heat off and leaving them to soak for 2 hours.

When you're ready to make the soup, first heat the oil in a large (6 pint/3.5 litre) saucepan, add the finely chopped onion and let it cook for about 10 minutes without colouring. Then add the garlic and cook for another minute. Now add the tomato purée and fresh rosemary, stir for a minute, and then pour in the beans, together with the water they were soaking in. Now bring everything up to simmering point, boil for 10 minutes and simmer gently for 1¼-1½ hours, or until the beans are tender.

After this time, season with salt and pepper, then pour half the soup into a blender, switch on and blend until it's absolutely smooth. Now return the puréed half to the pan to join the rest of the beans, bring back to a gentle simmer, then add the macaroni and simmer for a further 10-12 minutes, stirring from time to time, until the macaroni is cooked. Serve in hot soup bowls with lots of the Parmesan sprinkled over.

Crostini Lazio
Serves 4-6 (makes 12)

For the crostini

1 small, thin French stick, cut into 12 slices about 1 inch (2.5 cm) thick, or 3 slices from a thick sliced loaf, cut into quarters

3 tablespoons olive oil

1 fat clove garlic, crushed

For the topping

4 oz (110 g) firm goats' cheese

4 oz (110 g) best-quality tuna in oil, in a tin or jar, drained, reserving 1 tablespoon of the oil

1 tablespoon salted capers or capers in vinegar, thoroughly rinsed and drained

1 tablespoon finely grated Parmesan

1 dessertspoon lemon juice

To garnish

12 caper berries, if you like

You will also need a baking tray, 10 x 14 inches (25.5 x 35.5 cm).

Pre-heat the oven to gas mark 4, 350°F (180°C).

This is my own interpretation of some crostini I was served in trattoria "Checchino" in Rome, a brilliant combination of tuna and goats' cheese. It was before England played Italy in a World Cup qualifier, so I decided to name it after Rome's football club!

For the crostini, drizzle the olive oil over the baking tray, add the garlic, then, using your hands, spread the oil and garlic over the surface of the baking tray. Next, place the slices of bread on top of the oil and turn them over so that both sides are lightly coated. Now bake them in the oven for 10-15 minutes, until crisp and crunchy, but put a timer on, as they soon overbake.

For the topping, just peel the rind off the goats' cheese, using a sharp knife, then cut the cheese into 4 pieces. Next, place all the ingredients, including the reserved oil, into a liquidiser or food processor and blend until the mixture is smooth. If making this ahead, cover and chill in the fridge till needed. Then remove it half an hour before serving and spread it on the crostini, topping each one with a caper berry, if using. Don't assemble them until the last minute, though, or the bread loses some of its crispness.

Pasta

Pasta Puttanesca
Serves 2

8 oz (225 g) dried spaghetti

For the sauce

1 lb (450 g) ripe, red tomatoes

2 tablespoons extra virgin olive oil

2 cloves garlic, finely chopped

1 fresh red chilli, deseeded
and chopped

1 dessertspoon chopped fresh
basil, plus extra chopped
fresh basil to serve

2 oz (50 g) tinned anchovies,
drained

6 oz (175 g) pitted black olives,
chopped

1 heaped tablespoon capers,
drained

1 rounded tablespoon
tomato purée

lots of freshly grated Parmesan,
to serve

freshly milled black pepper

In Italian, a *puttanesca* is a 'lady of the night', which is why at home we always refer to this recipe as 'tart's spaghetti'. Presumably the sauce has adopted this name because it's hot, strong and gutsy – anyway, eating it is a highly pleasurable experience. If you are a strict vegetarian, replace the anchovies with another heaped tablespoon of capers.

First of all, skin the tomatoes by pouring boiling water over them and leaving them for 1 minute exactly. Then drain off the water and, as soon as they are cool enough to handle, slip off their skins and chop the tomatoes.

To make the sauce, heat the oil in a medium saucepan, then add the garlic, chilli and basil and cook these briefly till the garlic is pale gold. Then add all the other sauce ingredients, stir and season with a little pepper – but no salt because of the anchovies. Turn the heat to low and let the sauce simmer very gently, without a lid, for 40 minutes, by which time it will have reduced to a lovely thick mass, with very little liquid left.

While the sauce is cooking, take your largest saucepan and cook the pasta (see page 129). After that, drain it in a colander, return it to the saucepan *presto pronto*, and toss the sauce in it, adding the extra basil. Mix thoroughly and serve in well heated bowls, with lots of grated Parmesan to sprinkle over – and have plenty of gutsy, 'tarty' Italian red wine to wash it down.

Penne Rigate with Classic Fresh Tomato Sauce and Mozzarella
Serves 2-3

12 oz (350 g) dried penne rigate

5 oz (150 g) mozzarella, cubed

a little finely grated Parmesan, to serve

a few whole basil leaves, to garnish

For the tomato sauce

2 lb 8 oz (1.15 kg) ripe, red tomatoes

1 tablespoon olive oil

1 medium onion, finely chopped

1 fat clove garlic, crushed

about 12 large leaves of fresh basil

salt and freshly milled black pepper

Although it's very simple, this classic tomato sauce reduces down to a very fresh, concentrated tomato flavour – one of the best sauces ever invented. It even freezes well.

To make the sauce, start by skinning the tomatoes. Pour boiling water over them and leave them for 1 minute exactly. Then drain off the water and, as soon as they are cool enough to handle, slip off their skins. Reserve 3 of the tomatoes for later and roughly chop the rest. Next, heat the oil in a medium saucepan, then add the onion and garlic and let them gently cook for 5-6 minutes, until they are softened and golden. Now add the chopped tomatoes with a third of the basil, torn into pieces. Add some salt and freshly milled black pepper, then all you do is let the tomatoes simmer over a very low heat, without a lid, for $1\frac{1}{2}$-$1\frac{3}{4}$ hours or until almost all the liquid has evaporated and the tomatoes are reduced to a thick, jam-like consistency, stirring now and then. Roughly chop the reserved tomatoes and stir them in, along with the rest of the basil leaves, also torn into pieces.

When you are ready to eat, gently re-heat the tomato sauce and put the pasta on to cook (see page 129). Stir the mozzarella into the sauce and let it simmer for 2-3 minutes, by which time the cheese will have begun to melt. Serve the sauce spooned over the drained pasta, sprinkled with Parmesan and add a few fresh basil leaves as a garnish.

Meatballs with Spaghetti and Classic Fresh Tomato Sauce
Serves 4 (makes 24 meatballs)

For the meatballs

8 oz (225 g) minced pork

1 dessertspoon chopped fresh sage

3½ oz (95 g) mortadella or unsmoked bacon

2 tablespoons freshly grated Parmesan

2 tablespoons chopped fresh parsley

3 oz (75 g) white bread, without crusts, soaked in 2 tablespoons milk

1 large egg

a little grated nutmeg

salt and freshly milled black pepper

To cook and serve

1 lb (450 g) dried spaghetti

1 quantity Classic Fresh Tomato Sauce (see page 39)

1-2 tablespoons groundnut or other flavourless oil, for frying

a little Parmesan

a few fresh basil leaves

The main criteria for any meatball is that it should have a kind of melt-in-the-mouth lightness and not be heavy and bouncy. These, I think, are just right.

To make the meatballs, all you do is place all the ingredients into the bowl of a food processor, season with salt and freshly milled black pepper, and blend everything on a low speed until thoroughly blended. If you don't have a processor, chop everything as finely as possible with a sharp knife and blend it with a fork. Now take walnut-sized pieces of the mixture and shape them into rounds – you should end up with 24 meatballs. Then put them in a large dish or on a tray, cover with clingfilm and chill for about 30 minutes to firm up.

Meanwhile, pre-heat the oven to a low setting to keep the meatballs warm. Then, when you are ready to cook them, heat 1 tablespoon of the oil in a large frying pan and, over a fairly high heat, add 12 meatballs at a time and cook them until they are crispy and brown all over, adding a little more oil as necessary. This will take 4-5 minutes per batch, so, as they are cooked, remove them to a plate and keep them warm, covered with foil, in the oven.

Meanwhile, cook the pasta (see page 129) and gently warm the tomato sauce. Then drain the pasta, return it to the pan and toss in the tomato sauce. Quickly mix well and then pile it on to plates. Top with the meatballs, sprinkle with some freshly grated Parmesan and finish with a few basil leaves.

Spaghetti with Olive Oil, Garlic and Chilli
Serves 2

8 oz (225 g) dried spaghetti
or linguine

4 tablespoons extra virgin olive oil

2 fat cloves garlic, finely chopped

1 fat red chilli, deseeded and finely
chopped

freshly milled black pepper

This one is pure pasta eaten and savoured for its own sake with the minimum amount
of adornment – just a hint of garlic, chilli and olive oil.

Begin by putting the pasta on to cook (see page 129). Then just heat the olive oil in a small
frying pan and, when it is hot, add the garlic, chilli and some freshly milled black pepper.
Cook these very gently for about 2 minutes, which will be enough time for the flavourings
to infuse the oil. When the pasta is cooked, return it to the saucepan after draining, then
pour in the hot oil. Mix well and serve straightaway on warmed pasta plates.

Lasagne al Forno
Serves 8

1 lb (450 g) green no-cook dried lasagne sheets (about 24 sheets)

1 quantity (2 lb 8 oz/1.15 kg) Classic Ragù (see page 46)

14 oz (400 g) mozzarella, diced

4 oz (110 g) Parmesan, freshly grated or shaved

For the cream sauce

2½ pints (1.5 litres) milk

6 oz (175 g) butter

4 oz (110 g) plain flour

6 fl oz (175 ml) double cream

¼ whole nutmeg

salt and freshly milled black pepper

You will also need a 10 x 12 x 3 inch (25.5 x 30 x 7.5 cm) ovenproof dish or roasting tin, well buttered.

Lasagne has suffered greatly from being anglicised, factory made and served as cheap nosh, its authenticity obliterated – all the more reason to reinvent this great classic dish in all its original glory.

First of all, make the cream sauce: place the milk, butter, flour and some seasoning in a large, thick-based saucepan. Place this over a gentle heat and whisk continuously with a balloon whisk until the sauce comes to simmering point and thickens. Then, with the heat as low as possible, continue to cook the sauce for about 10 minutes.

After that, sieve the sauce into a bowl, beat in the cream, taste and season if it needs it, and grate in the nutmeg. Now spread about a quarter of the ragù over the base of the dish or tin. Cover this with one-fifth of the sauce, followed by a quarter of the mozzarella, then arrange a single layer (about 6 sheets) of the lasagne on top. (I find you need 4 placed side by side lengthways and the other 2 halved and spread along the gap that's left.) Repeat this process 3 more times, finishing with a final layer of sauce, then cover the whole lot with the grated or shaved Parmesan and the lasagne is ready for the oven. All this can be done well in advance. Then, when you're ready to bake the lasagne, pre-heat the oven to gas mark 4, 350°F (180°C) and pop the lasagne on to the top shelf of the oven for 45-50 minutes, or until it's bubbling and turning slightly golden on top.

Classic Ragù
Makes 2 lb 8 oz (1.15 kg)

4 tablespoons extra virgin olive oil

1 large onion, finely chopped

7 oz (200 g) sliced pancetta

2 fat cloves garlic, chopped

12 oz (350 g) minced beef

12 oz (350 g) minced pork

6 oz (175 g) chicken livers

1 x 400 g tin Italian chopped tomatoes, and 1 x 230 g tin chopped tomatoes

6 tablespoons tomato purée

6 fl oz (175 ml) red wine

¼ whole nutmeg

⅓ oz (15 g) fresh basil

salt and freshly milled black pepper

You will also need a 6 pint (3.5 litre) flameproof casserole.

Pre-heat the oven to gas mark 1, 275°F (140°C).

This is the ragù to use in the Lasagne al Forno (see page 44). It can be used for other recipes, too, including the cannelloni on page 61. If I am not making the lasagne and don't need it all in one go, I divide the ragù into 8 oz (225 g) packs for the freezer, each of which is enough to serve two with spaghetti.

First of all, heat a tablespoon of the oil in your largest frying pan over a medium heat and gently fry the onion for about 10 minutes, moving it around from time to time. While it is softening, chop the pancetta: the best way to do this is to roll it into a sausage shape, then, using a sharp knife, slice it lengthways into 4, then slice the lengths across as finely as possible. After the 10 minutes are up, add this to the pan, along with the garlic, and continue cooking the whole lot for about 5 minutes. Now transfer this mixture to the casserole. Next, add another tablespoon of oil to the pan, turn up the heat to its highest, then add the minced beef and brown it, breaking it up and moving it around in the pan. (A wooden fork is really helpful here.) When the beef is browned, tip it into the casserole to join the onion mixture, then heat another tablespoon of oil and do exactly the same with the minced pork.

While the pork is browning, trim the chicken livers, rinse them under cold, running water and dry them thoroughly with kitchen paper. Pull off any skin and snip out any tubes or odd bits of fat with kitchen scissors, then chop the livers minutely small. When the pork is browned, transfer it to the casserole, too. Finally, heat the remaining tablespoon of oil and cook the pieces of chicken liver, adding these to the casserole as soon as they have browned nicely. After that, you need to remove the pan and place the casserole over the direct heat, and give everything a really good stir. Then add the contents of both tins of tomatoes, the tomato purée, red wine, a really good seasoning of salt and freshly milled black pepper and grate in the nutmeg. More stirring now, then allow this to come up to simmering point. While that happens, strip the leaves from half the basil, tear them into small pieces and add them to the casserole.

Then, as soon as everything is simmering, place the casserole on the centre shelf of the oven and leave it to cook slowly, without a lid, for exactly 4 hours.

It's a good idea to have a look after 3 hours to make sure all is well and to have a good stir, but what you should end up with is a thick, reduced, concentrated sauce, with only a trace of liquid left in it. When that happens, remove the casserole from the oven, taste to check the seasoning, then strip the remaining leaves off the basil, tear them into small pieces and stir them in.

Orecchiette with Sprouting Broccoli, Pine Nuts and Sultanas
Serves 4

12 oz (350 g) dried orecchiette

1 lb (450 g) sprouting broccoli

3 tablespoons pine nuts

3 tablespoons sultanas

4 tablespoons olive oil

1 medium onion, thinly sliced

4 tinned anchovy fillets, drained and chopped

salt and freshly ground black pepper

freshly grated Pecorino Romano, to serve

Orecchiette in Italian means 'little ears' and while they are a very special pasta shape, which catches the sauce perfectly, they are not always available, so any other pasta shape can be used. It's also worth noting that this is much much nicer that it sounds!

First of all, put a large pan of water on to boil for the pasta. Then put the sultanas in a small bowl, cover with cold water and leave them to soak for 5 minutes so they plump up. Meanwhile, trim the tough, fibrous ends off the sprouting broccoli and then slice the stems into short, $\frac{1}{2}$ inch (1 cm) lengths, dividing up some of the larger heads of broccoli as you want them to be the same size as the pasta. Transfer the sprouting broccoli to a steamer, sprinkle with salt and cover and steam for 7 minutes. Then remove the steamer from the pan and leave aside, covered. Now quickly add the water from the steamer pan to the pasta pan and bring it back to boiling point to cook the pasta (see page 129).

While the pasta is cooking, heat the oil in a large frying pan and gently fry the sliced onion for 3 or 4 minutes. Then throw in the pine nuts and sultanas (drain them first) and continue to cook gently until the onion is softened and the pine nuts lightly browned. Now add the chopped anchovy fillets, and as soon as they have melted into the mix, the sauce is ready. Add the steamed broccoli and briefly toss everything together. Then drain the pasta, return it to the hot, dry pan you cooked it in and toss it with the broccoli mixture. Season to taste and serve immediately with plenty of freshly grated Pecorino Romano.

Sicilian Pasta with Roasted Tomatoes and Aubergines
Serves 2

8 oz (225 g) dried spaghetti

12 large tomatoes
(about 2 lb/900 g)

1 large aubergine, cut into
1 inch (2.5 cm) cubes

2 large cloves garlic,
finely chopped

about 3-4 tablespoons olive oil

12 large basil leaves, torn in half,
plus a few extra, to garnish

5 oz (150 g) mozzarella, cut into
½ inch (1 cm) cubes

salt and freshly milled
black pepper

You will also need two
10 x 14 inch (25.5 x 35.5 cm)
baking trays.

Pre-heat the oven to gas mark 6,
400°F (200°C).

Aubergines, tomatoes and mozzarella are the traditional ingredients of any classic Sicilian sauce for pasta, and roasting the tomatoes and aubergines to get them slightly charred adds an extra flavour dimension.

First of all, place the aubergine cubes in a colander, sprinkle them with salt and leave them to stand for half an hour, weighed down with something heavy to squeeze out the excess juices.

Meanwhile, skin the tomatoes by pouring boiling water over them and leaving them for 1 minute, then drain off the water and, as soon as they are cool enough to handle, slip off the skins. Cut each tomato in half and place the halves on one of the baking trays, cut side uppermost, then season with salt and freshly milled black pepper. Sprinkle over the chopped garlic, distributing it evenly among the tomatoes, and follow this with a few drops of olive oil on each one. Top each tomato half with half a basil leaf, turning each piece of leaf over to give it a good coating of oil. Place the baking tray on the middle shelf of the oven and roast the tomatoes for 50-60 minutes, or until the edges are slightly blackened.

Meanwhile, drain the aubergines and squeeze out as much excess juice as possible. Dry them thoroughly with a clean cloth and place them on the other baking tray. Then drizzle 1 tablespoon of the olive oil all over the aubergines and place them on the top shelf of the oven, above the tomatoes, to roast for half an hour.

Towards the end of the cooking time, cook the pasta (see page 129). When the tomatoes and aubergines are ready, scrape them, along with all their lovely cooking juices, into a saucepan and place it over a low heat, then add the cubed mozzarella and stir gently. Now drain the pasta, pile it into a warm bowl, spoon the tomato and aubergine mixture over the top and scatter over a few basil leaves.

Linguine with Mussels and Walnut Parsley Pesto
Serves 2

6 oz (175 g) dried linguine

2 lb (900 g) mussels, cleaned and prepared

1 tablespoon olive oil

1 shallot, chopped

1 clove garlic, chopped

6 fl oz (175 ml) dry white wine

2 tablespoons chopped fresh flat-leaf parsley, to serve

salt and freshly milled black pepper

For the pesto

½ oz (10 g) walnuts, chopped

1 oz (25 g) fresh flat-leaf parsley

2 tablespoons olive oil

1 clove garlic, peeled

salt and freshly milled black pepper

For me, mussels are still a luxury food that cost very little money. I don't think anything can match their exquisite, fresh-from-the-sea flavour. In this recipe every precious drop of mussel juice is used, which gives a lovely, concentrated flavour. Now that mussels come ready cleaned and prepared, it makes the whole thing very simple and easy: all you have to do is put them in plenty of cold water, then pull off any beardy strands with a small, sharp knife. Use the mussels as soon as possible and discard any that don't close tightly when given a sharp tap.

First, prepare the pesto: select a large pan that will hold the mussels comfortably, then in it heat 1 tablespoon of the olive oil and sauté the walnuts in the hot oil to get them nicely toasted on all sides – this will take 1-2 minutes. Place the walnuts and any oil left in the pan into a blender or food processor, add the parsley and garlic, the remaining tablespoon of oil and seasoning, then blend everything to make a purée.

Next, you need to deal with the mussels: heat the tablespoon of olive oil in the same pan that you sautéed the walnuts in, add the shallot and chopped garlic and cook these over a medium heat for about 5 minutes or until they're just soft. Now turn the heat up high, tip in the prepared mussels and add the wine and some salt and pepper. Put on a close-fitting lid, turn the heat down to medium and cook the mussels for 5 minutes, shaking the pan once or twice or until they have all opened. Discard any that remain closed. During those 5 minutes, bring a large pan of water up to the boil for the pasta (see page 129). Then, when the mussels are cooked, remove them from the heat and transfer them to a warm bowl, using a slotted spoon and shaking each one well so that no juice is left inside. Keep 8 mussels aside still in their shells for a garnish. Then remove the rest from their shells and keep them warm, covered with foil, in a low oven. Next, place a sieve lined with muslin or gauze over a bowl and strain the mussel liquor through it. This is very important as it removes any bits of sand or grit that get lodged in the mussel shells.

Now it's time to put the pasta on to cook. Meanwhile, pour the strained mussel liquor back into the original saucepan and fast-boil to reduce it by about one-third. After that, turn the heat to low and stir in the pesto. Now add the shelled mussels to the pesto sauce and remove it from the heat. As soon as the pasta is cooked, quickly strain it in a colander and divide it between 2 hot pasta bowls.

Spoon the mussels and pesto over each portion, add the mussels in their shells, and scatter over the chopped parsley. Serve absolutely immediately with some well chilled white wine. Yummy!

Pasta with Four Cheeses
Serves 2

8 oz (225 g) dried penne rigate

2 oz (50 g) ricotta

3 oz (75 g) Torta Gorgonzola, diced

1 oz (25 g) Pecorino Romano, finely grated, plus a little extra to serve

2 tablespoons snipped fresh chives

I know you can see only three cheeses in the recipe, but there is a hidden one, because Torta Gorgonzola is in fact made from layers of two cheeses: Gorgonzola and mascarpone. Add to that ricotta and some Pecorino and you have a five-star recipe – including the best-quality pasta, of course! If you can't find Torta Gorgonzola, there is a very similar layered cheese called Torta di Dolcelatte, which you could use instead.

You need to start this by measuring out the cheeses on a plate to have them at the ready, then cook the pasta in plenty of boiling water for 1 minute less than the full cooking time – you need to know your pasta (see page 129).

As soon as it's ready, drain the pasta in a colander and immediately return it to the saucepan so that it still has quite a bit of moisture clinging to it. Now quickly add the chives, ricotta, Torta Gorgonzola and Pecorino Romano, and stir till the cheese begins to melt. Serve it in hot bowls with the extra Pecorino on the table to sprinkle over.

Spaghetti alla Carbonara
Serves 2

8 oz (225 g) dried spaghetti

5 oz (150 g) smoked pancetta, cubed or sliced

2 large eggs, plus 2 extra yolks

1½ tablespoons extra virgin olive oil

4 tablespoons Pecorino Romano, finely grated, plus extra to serve

4 tablespoons double cream

freshly milled black pepper

This is my favourite, and the very best version I know of the great classic Italian recipe for pasta with bacon and egg sauce. I used to make it with English bacon and Parmesan cheese, but now we are able to get Italian pancetta and Pecorino Romano cheese, it is a great improvement.

First of all, cook the pasta (see page 129). Meanwhile, heat the olive oil in a frying pan and fry the pancetta until it's crisp and golden, about 5 minutes. Next, whisk the eggs, yolks, cheese and cream in a bowl and season generously with black pepper.

Then, when the pasta is cooked, drain it quickly in a colander, leaving a little of the moisture still clinging. Now quickly return it to the saucepan and add the pancetta and any oil in the pan, along with the egg and cream mixture. Stir very thoroughly, so that everything gets a good coating – what happens is that the liquid egg cooks briefly as it comes into contact with the hot pasta. Serve the pasta on really hot deep plates with some extra grated Pecorino.

Baked Cannelloni
Serves 4

8 fresh lasagne sheets
(about 6 oz/175 g)

a 4½ oz (125g) ball of mozzarella

1½ oz (40 g) finely grated
Parmesan, plus a little extra,
to serve

For the ragù

(see page 46 and recipe method,
right)

For the béchamel sauce

1 pint (570 ml) milk

2 oz (50 g) butter

1¼ oz (35 g) plain flour

1 bay leaf

a good grating of whole nutmeg

2½ fl oz (65 ml) double cream

salt and freshly milled
black pepper

You will also need a baking dish,
7 x 9 inches (18 x 23 cm), buttered.

I have discovered that the best way to make this excellent supper dish is to buy fresh sheets of lasagne that don't need pre-cooking.

You will need 1 lb (450 g) of ragù for this recipe, but it is worth making the whole quantity on page 46 as it freezes well.

To make the cannelloni, first make a béchamel sauce by placing the milk, butter, flour, bay leaf, nutmeg and seasoning into a medium saucepan over a medium heat, then, whisking all the time, slowly bring it up to simmering point until the sauce has thickened. Then turn the heat down to its lowest setting and let the sauce simmer for about 5 minutes. After that, remove the bay leaf, stir in the cream, taste to check the seasoning, cover, and leave aside.

Now pre-heat the oven to gas mark 4, 350°F (180°C), then cut the lasagne sheets in half so that you have 16 pieces, each measuring 4½ x 3 inches (11 x 7.5 cm). Next, cut the ball of mozzarella in half and then cut each half into eight pieces, and place a piece of mozzarella on each piece of lasagne. Then divide the ragù among the sheets and roll them up, starting from one of the shorter edges. As you do this, arrange them in the baking dish with the join underneath – what you should have are 2 rows neatly fitting together lengthways in the dish. Now pour the béchamel sauce over the cannelloni and scatter the Parmesan over that. Place the dish on the centre shelf of the oven to bake for 40 minutes, by which time it should be golden brown and bubbling. Then remove it from the oven and let it settle for about 10 minutes. Serve with extra Parmesan to sprinkle over.

Trofie Pasta Liguria
Serves 2

6 oz (175 g) dried trofie pasta

3 oz (75 g) fine green beans
or fresh, shelled peas

3 oz (75 g) Anya or other small
salad potatoes

grated Parmesan or Pecorino
Romano, to serve

For the pesto

2 oz (50 g) fresh basil leaves

1 large clove garlic, crushed

1 tablespoon pine nuts

6 tablespoons extra virgin olive oil

1 oz (25 g) grated Parmesan
or Pecorino Romano

salt

I have given this dish this particular name because I have often eaten it in one of my favourite Italian restaurants in Portofino. To save time, you could use a 120 g tub of fresh pesto sauce. Trofie is a Ligurian pasta shape but any other pasta will work just as well.

First, make the pesto. If you have a blender, put the basil, garlic, pine nuts and olive oil together with some salt, in the goblet and blend until you have a smooth purée. Then transfer the purée to a bowl and stir in the grated Parmesan or Pecorino Romano cheese.

If you don't have a blender, use a large pestle and mortar to pound the basil, garlic and pine nuts to a paste. Slowly add the cheese, then very gradually add the oil until you have obtained a smooth purée, and season with salt to taste.

Next, heat some pasta bowls ready for serving and put the pasta on to cook (see page 129). Meanwhile, if you are using beans, trim and cut them into lengths, about 1½ inches (4 cm). Wash and slice the potatoes next, leaving the skins on; they need to be fractionally thicker than a 50p coin.

After the pasta has been cooking for 10 minutes, throw in the beans and potatoes. (If using peas, give them slightly less cooking time.) Now give the ingredients another stir and bring the water back to the boil, then set a timer for 8 minutes. After that, drain the pasta, potatoes and beans (or peas) in a colander, not completely, as it needs a little water still clinging to it. Then tip everything back into the saucepan, add the pesto sauce, and stir it pretty niftily to give everything a good coating. Finally, serve in the hot pasta bowls with the extra Parmesan or Pecorino Romano in a bowl to sprinkle over.

Penne with Wild Mushrooms and Mascarpone Sauce
Serves 4-6

1 lb 2 oz (500 g) dried penne rigate

½ oz (10 g) dried porcini mushrooms

1 lb (450 g) mixed fresh mushrooms (eg, flat, chestnut, or mixed wild mushrooms), finely chopped

9 oz (250 g) mascarpone

4 large shallots, finely chopped

2 oz (50 g) butter

2 tablespoons balsamic vinegar

⅓ whole nutmeg

lots of grated Parmesan, to serve

salt and freshly milled black pepper

This recipe has all those delectable, concentrated mushroom flavours, with the added bonus of some luscious, creamy mascarpone.

First, pop the porcini into a small bowl with 3 tablespoons of boiling water and leave them to soak for 30 minutes. Then heat the butter in a medium frying pan over a gentle heat, stir in the shallots and let them cook gently for 5 minutes.

Next, strain the porcini into a sieve lined with a double sheet of kitchen paper, reserving the soaking liquid and squeezing the porcini dry. Then chop them finely and add them to the pan, along with the fresh mushrooms and the balsamic vinegar. Next, season with salt and pepper and grate in the nutmeg. Give it all a good stir, then cook gently, uncovered, for 30-40 minutes, until all the liquid has evaporated.

About 15 minutes before the mushrooms are ready, put the pasta on to cook (see page 129). Then, 2 minutes before it is cooked, mix the mascarpone – reserving 1 tablespoon – with the mushrooms and the mushroom soaking liquid, and warm through.

Drain the pasta in a colander, return it to the hot pan and quickly mix in the mushroom mixture, then take it to the table in a hot serving bowl with the rest of the mascarpone melting on top, and the Parmesan handed round separately.

Risotto
gnocchi

Risotto alla Milanese
Serves 4

carnaroli rice, measured
to the 12 fl oz (340 ml) level in
a measuring jug

4 oz (110 g) butter

½ teaspoon saffron stamens

1 medium onion, chopped small

2 tablespoons bone marrow,
if liked – you need an obliging
butcher for this one

3 fl oz (75 ml) dry white wine

about 2 pints (1.2 litres) simmering
chicken stock

4 tablespoons freshly grated
Parmesan, plus extra to serve

salt and freshly milled
black pepper

This is my version of the great Italian classic and the best accompaniment of all to Ossobuco (see page 93). The traditional risotto method demands your full attention, so if you are serving this to guests, have them bring their apéritifs and join you around the stove. If you want to be free, you can make a cheats' version using the oven method described on pages 77 and 81. Don't worry if bone marrow is not available, it will still be extremely good.

Begin by melting half the butter in a heavy-based, medium saucepan, add the saffron and allow 1 minute for the heat to draw out the flavour. Then add the chopped onion and bone marrow and cook, over a low heat, uncovered, for about 10 minutes until softened. Stir in the rice and cook for a minute or two before adding the wine and some salt. Stir gently once, then simmer over a low heat, without a lid, until the liquid has been absorbed (about 4-5 minutes). Now put in a ladleful of the simmering stock and again, let it simmer until the stock has nearly all been absorbed but the rice is still moist. Continue adding the boiling stock, a ladleful at a time, until the rice is tender but still creamy (about 30 minutes). There should still be a very little liquid visible – the risotto should be soupy rather than mushy. Stir as necessary to prevent the rice from sticking to the bottom of the pan – particularly towards the end.

When the rice is cooked, remove the pan from the heat and stir in the remaining butter and the Parmesan. Cover and leave to stand, off the heat, for 5 minutes before serving. Season to taste, then serve with lots more freshly grated Parmesan on the table.

Semolina Gnocchi with Gorgonzola
Serves 3-4

5 oz (150 g) semolina

2 oz (50 g) Gorgonzola Piccante, chopped into small dice

10 fl oz (275 ml) milk

freshly grated nutmeg

2½ oz (60 g) Parmesan, finely grated

2 large eggs

2 oz (50 g) ricotta

salt and freshly milled black pepper

You will also need a non-stick baking tin, 6 x 10 x 1 inches (15 x 25.5 x 2.5 cm), lined with baking parchment, a 2 inch (5 cm) pastry cutter, and an ovenproof baking dish, 7½ x 7½ x 2 inches (19 x 19 x 5 cm), lightly buttered.

These gnocchi are made with semolina instead of the usual potato. They are equally charming, with crisp, baked edges, and are light and fluffy on the inside. Remember, though, that the mixture needs to be prepared the day before you want to serve the gnocchi.

First of all, you'll need a large saucepan, and into that put the milk and 10 fl oz (275 ml) water, along with a good grating of nutmeg, 1 teaspoon salt and some freshly milled black pepper. Then sprinkle in the semolina and, over a medium heat and stirring constantly with a wooden spoon, bring it all up to the boil. Let the mixture bubble gently for about 4 minutes, still stirring, until it is thick enough to stand the spoon up in, then remove the pan from the heat and beat in 2 oz (50 g) of the Parmesan and the eggs. Now adjust the seasoning, then pour the mixture into the prepared tin and spread it out evenly with a spatula. When it's absolutely cold, cover the tin with clingfilm and leave it in the fridge overnight to firm up.

When you are ready to cook the gnocchi, pre-heat the oven to gas mark 6, 400°F (200°C). Turn the cheese and semolina mixture out on to a board, peel away the baking parchment, and cut the mixture into 2 inch (5 cm) rounds with the pastry cutter, then reshape the trimmings and cut out more rounds until the mixture is all used up. I quite like rounds, but if you prefer, you can cut out squares or triangles – it makes no difference. Place them, slightly overlapping, in the baking dish, then dot with the ricotta and sprinkle over the Gorgonzola, followed by the rest of the Parmesan. Bake on a high shelf of the oven for 30 minutes, until the gnocchi are golden brown and the cheese is bubbling.

Spinach Gnocchi with Five Cheeses
Serves 4 as a starter or 2 as a main course

8 oz (225 g) young leaf spinach

6 oz (175 g) ricotta

2 oz (50 g) mascarpone

2 oz (50 g) creamy Gorgonzola, roughly cubed

2 oz (50 g) fontina or Gruyère, cut into small cubes

2 oz (50 g) Pecorino Romano, finely grated

1 medium King Edward potato (about 6 oz/175 g)

a little freshly grated nutmeg

1 oz (25 g) plain flour, plus a little extra for rolling

1 large egg

1 heaped tablespoon freshly snipped chives

salt and freshly milled black pepper

You will also need a 7 x 10 inch (18 x 25.5 cm), shallow, ovenproof dish.

These gnocchi are little dumplings made from potatoes, flour and egg. I dream about eating this recipe on a warm, sunny summer's day outside, but in winter it's still an excellent lunch for two people or as a first course for four. For a variation, instead of using all cheese, halve the amount and add 6 oz (175 g) of crisp, crumbly bacon or pancetta. Make these gnocchi the day you are going to serve them because they will discolour if left overnight.

First, boil the potato, leaving the skin on, which will take about 25 minutes. Meanwhile, pick over the spinach, remove the stalks, then rinse the leaves. Place them in a large saucepan over a medium heat and cook briefly, with a lid on, for 1-2 minutes, until they're wilted and collapsed down. Then drain in a colander and, when cool enough to handle, squeeze all the moisture out and chop finely.

When the potato is cooked, drain and, holding it in a clean tea cloth, peel off the skin and sieve the potato into a bowl. Next, add the spinach, ricotta, nutmeg and flour to join the potato, then beat the egg and add half, along with some seasoning. Now, gently and lightly, using a fork, bring the mixture together. Finish off with your hands and knead the mixture lightly into a soft dough, adding 1 teaspoonful or more of the beaten egg if it is a little dry. Then transfer the mixture to a floured surface and divide it into 4. Roll each quarter into a sausage shape approximately ½ inch (1 cm) in diameter, then cut it on the diagonal into 1 inch (2.5 cm) pieces, placing them on a tray or plate as they are cut. Cover with clingfilm and chill for at least 30 minutes, but longer won't matter. After that, using a fork with the prongs facing upwards, press the fork down on to one side of each gnocchi so that it leaves a row of ridges on each one; at the same time, ease them into crescent shapes. The ridges are there to absorb the sauce effectively. Now cover and chill the gnocchi again until you are ready to cook them.

To cook the gnocchi, have all the cheeses ready. Pre-heat the grill to its highest setting, then bring a large, shallow pan of approximately 6 pints (3.5 litres) water up to simmering point and put the serving dish near the grill to warm through. Now drop the gnocchi into the water and cook them for 3 minutes; they will start to float to the surface after about 2 minutes, but they need an extra minute. When they are ready, remove them with a draining spoon and transfer them straight to the serving dish. When they are all in, quickly stir in first the mascarpone and chives, then sprinkle in the Gorgonzola and fontina, then add some seasoning and cover the whole lot with the grated Pecorino. Now pop it under the grill for 3-4 minutes, until it is golden brown and bubbling. Serve absolutely immediately on hot plates.

Tiger Prawn Risotto with Lobster Sauce
Serves 4 as a starter or 2 as a main course

6 oz (175 g) cooked peeled tiger prawns or any other medium-sized prawns, defrosted if frozen, or 7 oz (200 g) squat lobster tails in brine, drained

carnaroli rice measured to the 6 fl oz (175 ml) level in a measuring jug

1 x 780 g jar lobster bisque or luxury fish soup

1½ oz (40 g) butter

1 medium onion, finely chopped

3 fl oz (75 ml) dry sherry

2 oz (50 g) fontina or Gruyère, finely grated, plus a little extra to serve

2 tablespoons whipping cream

a few sprigs of fresh watercress, to garnish

salt and freshly milled black pepper

You will also need an ovenproof baking dish, 7 x 7 x 2 inches (18 x 18 x 5 cm).

Pre-heat the oven to gas mark 2, 300°F (150°C).

Risottos with seafood abound all along the Italian coast but, alas, the fish of the Mediterranean are not that forthcoming here. However, this goes some way to recapturing the memory and is extremely good.

First of all, place the baking dish in the oven to pre-heat. Meanwhile, in a large frying pan, melt the butter and, over a medium heat, sauté the onion for 7-8 minutes, until soft. Now stir the rice into the buttery juices so it gets a good coating, then pour in the lobster bisque, or soup, and sherry and season. Give it a good stir and bring it up to simmering point, then pour the whole lot into the baking dish and return it to the oven, uncovered, for 35 minutes.

Towards the end of the cooking time, pre-heat the grill to its highest setting. Take the risotto from the oven, taste to check the seasoning, then add the prawns (or lobster tails). Next, scatter the cheese over the top and drizzle the cream over. Now place the dish under the grill for 2-3 minutes, until the cheese is brown and bubbling, then serve immediately, garnished with the watercress and the extra cheese sprinkled over.

Gnocchi with Sage, Butter and Parmesan

Serves 4 as a starter or 2 as a main course

10 oz (275 g) King Edward potatoes (about 2 medium potatoes)

3½ oz (95 g) plain flour, sifted, plus a little extra for rolling

1 large egg, lightly beaten

3-4 tablespoons freshly grated Parmesan, to serve

salt and freshly milled black pepper

For the sauce

8 fresh sage leaves

2 oz (50 g) butter

1 large clove garlic, crushed

You will also need a shallow, ovenproof serving dish, about 7 x 10 inches (18 x 25.5 cm).

This recipe is very simple, served with just butter, sage and Parmesan. Make the gnocchi the day you are going to serve them, because they will discolour if left overnight.

First, place the potatoes in a suitably sized saucepan, almost cover with boiling water, add some salt, then put a lid on and simmer for 20-25 minutes, until tender. Drain well and, holding them in your hand with a tea cloth, quickly pare off the skins, using a potato peeler. Place the potatoes in a large bowl and, using an electric hand whisk on a slow speed, start to break the potatoes up, then increase the speed and gradually whisk until smooth and fluffy. Now let them cool. Next, add the sifted flour, along with half the beaten egg, season lightly and, using a fork, bring the mixture together. Then, using your hands, knead the mixture lightly to a soft dough – you may need to add a teaspoonful or so more of the egg if it is a little dry. Now transfer the mixture to a lightly floured surface, flour your hands and divide it into quarters. Then roll each quarter into a sausage shape about ½ inch (1 cm) in diameter, then cut it, on the diagonal, into 1 inch (2.5 cm) pieces, placing them on a tray or plate as they are cut. Cover with clingfilm and chill for at least 30 minutes. After that, using a fork with the prongs facing upwards, press the fork down on to one side of each gnocchi so that it leaves a row of ridges on each one; at the same time, ease them into crescent shapes. Now cover and chill the gnocchi again until you are ready to cook them.

To cook the gnocchi, firstly bring a large, shallow pan of approximately 6 pints (3.5 litres) of water to a simmer and put the serving dish in a low oven to warm through. Then drop the gnocchi into the water and cook for about 3 minutes; they will start to float to the surface after about 2 minutes, but they need 3 altogether. When they are ready, remove the gnocchi with a draining spoon and transfer them to the warm serving dish.

For the sauce, melt the butter with the garlic over a gentle heat until the garlic turns nut brown in colour – this will take about 1 minute. Next, add the sage leaves and allow the butter to froth while the sage leaves turn crisp – this will take about 30 seconds – then spoon the butter mixture over the warm gnocchi. Sprinkle half the Parmesan over and serve the rest separately.

Wild Mushroom Risotto
Serves 6 as a starter or 3 as a main course

½ oz (10 g) dried porcini mushrooms

8 oz (225 g) fresh, dark-gilled mushrooms

2½ oz (60 g) butter

1 medium onion, finely chopped

carnaroli rice measured to the 6 fl oz (175 ml) level in a measuring jug

5 fl oz (150 ml) dry Madeira

2 tablespoons freshly grated Parmesan, plus 2 oz (50 g) extra, shaved into flakes

salt and freshly milled black pepper

You will also need a shallow, ovenproof dish, 9 x 9 x 2 inches (23 x 23 x 5 cm), with a capacity of 2½ pints (1.5 litres).

I got a lot of flack from the purists when I first published this recipe, but my friend and fellow cookery writer Anna Del Conte reassured me by explaining that in Liguria they do sometimes cook risotto in the oven. So all is well.

First, you need to soak the dried mushrooms and, to do this, you place them in a bowl and pour 1 pint (570 ml) boiling water over them. Then just leave them to soak and soften for half an hour. Meanwhile, chop the fresh mushrooms into ½ inch (1 cm) chunks – not too small, as they shrink down in the cooking. Now melt the butter in a medium saucepan, add the onion and let it cook over a gentle heat for about 5 minutes, then add the fresh mushrooms, stir well and leave on one side while you deal with the porcini.

When they have had their half-hour soak, place a sieve over a bowl, line the sieve with a double sheet of kitchen paper and strain the mushrooms, reserving the liquid. Squeeze any excess liquid out of them, then chop them finely and transfer to the pan to join the other mushrooms and the onion. Keep the heat low and let the onions and mushrooms sweat gently (without a lid) and release their juices – which will take about 20 minutes. Meanwhile, pre-heat the oven to gas mark 2, 300°F (150°C) and put the dish in the oven to warm.

Now add the rice to the pan and stir it around to get a good coating of butter, then add the Madeira, followed by the strained mushroom soaking liquid. Add 1 teaspoon salt and some freshly milled black pepper, bring up to simmering point, then transfer the whole lot from the pan to the warmed dish. Stir once, then place it on the centre shelf of the oven without covering. Set a timer and give it 20 minutes exactly. After that, gently stir in the grated Parmesan, turning the rice grains over. Now put the timer on again and give it a further 15 minutes, then remove from the oven and put a clean tea cloth over it while you invite everyone to be seated. Like soufflés, risottos won't wait, so serve *presto pronto* on warmed plates and sprinkle with the shaved Parmesan.

Roman Gnocchi
with Classic Fresh Tomato Sauce
Serves 3-4

5 oz (150 g) semolina

5 oz (150 g) Parmesan,
freshly grated

10 fl oz (275 ml) milk

freshly grated nutmeg

3 oz (75 g) butter

2 large eggs, lightly beaten

salt and freshly milled
black pepper

To serve

½ quantity of Classic Fresh Tomato
Sauce (see page 39)

You will also need a non-stick
baking tin, 6 x 10 x 1 inches
(15 x 25.5 x 2.5 cm), lined with
baking parchment, a 2 inch (5 cm)
pastry cutter, and a 7 x 7 x 2 inch
(18 x 18 x 5 cm) shallow gratin
dish, buttered.

These little rounds made with cheese and semolina are baked in the oven with butter. Simple, inexpensive but really good. They are wonderful served with a fresh, classic tomato sauce – you will only need half the quantity of the recipe on page 39 but the other half will freeze well.

Begin by putting the milk and 10 fl oz (275 ml) water into a large saucepan, together with a good grating of nutmeg, 1 teaspoon of salt and some pepper. Now sprinkle in the semolina and, over a medium heat, bring it all to the boil, stirring constantly with a wooden spoon. Let the mixture bubble gently for about 4 minutes, still stirring, until it is thick enough to stand a spoon up in. Then remove the pan from the heat and beat in 1 oz (25 g) of the butter, 3 oz (75 g) of the Parmesan and the eggs. Adjust the seasoning, then pour the mixture into the prepared tin and, using a spatula, spread it out evenly. Then leave to cool and, when completely cold, cover the tin with clingfilm and leave it in the fridge overnight to firm up.

When you're ready to cook the gnocchi, pre-heat the oven to gas mark 6, 400°F (200°C). Then turn the cheese and semolina mixture out on to a board, peel away the parchment paper and cut the cheese and semolina into 2 inch (5 cm) rounds with the pastry cutter (or cut into 'fingers'). Reshape the trimmings and cut out more rounds until all the mixture is used up. Place them, slightly overlapping, in the gratin dish, then dot the top of the gnocchi with the remaining 2 oz (50 g) of butter and bake for 10 minutes.

Next, sprinkle the remaining 2 oz (50 g) of Parmesan over them and place the dish on an upper shelf of the oven and bake for a further 30 minutes or until the whole thing is golden brown and bubbling nicely. You might think this seems too much butter, but when serving it should be soaked in melted butter. Not for slimmers or the health-conscious, but wonderful. Gently warm the tomato sauce and serve with the gnocchi.

Fish
Meat

Veal Saltimbocca
Serves 2

2 veal escalopes (about 4 oz/110 g each); alternatively, use pork

4 slices Parma ham (about 2½ oz/60 g)

4 large fresh sage leaves

6 fl oz (175 ml) Marsala

1½ tablespoons olive oil

salt and freshly milled black pepper

You will also need a large, 9 inch (23 cm) frying pan, and 2 cocktail sticks.

Saltimbocca, which means 'jump in the mouth', is a classic Italian dish made with thin, battened-out slices of veal, which have Parma ham and sage leaves attached. These are quickly sautéed and then the whole thing is finished with a rich, dark Marsala-wine sauce.

First of all, cut each veal escalope into 2 pieces, then beat the pieces of meat out to make them a little thinner. Lay them out on a chopping board with a large piece of clingfilm on top and gently beat the meat out, using a rolling pin. Don't go mad and break the meat – it just needs to be flattened and stretched a bit. Season the meat with salt and pepper and now lay the slices of Parma ham on top of it (because they won't be precisely the same size, fold the ham and double over the pieces, if necessary, to make them fit). Now place a sage leaf in the centre of each piece and secure it with half a cocktail stick, using it as you would a dressmaking pin.

Next, measure the Marsala into a small saucepan and place it on a gentle heat to warm through. Now heat the oil in the frying pan until fairly hot, then fry the slices of veal (sage leaf side down first) for 2 minutes, then flip the pieces over and fry them for another minute. After that, pour in the hot Marsala and let it bubble and reduce for a couple of minutes or so until it becomes a syrupy sauce. Now transfer the veal to warm serving plates, remove the cocktail sticks and spoon the sauce over. Serve with sautéed potatoes, sprinkled with a few herbs before cooking, and a mixed salad.

Oven-baked Fish with Potatoes
Serves 2-3

1 lb (450 g) cod fillet, skinned

1 lb 4 oz (570 g) Desirée
or King Edward potatoes

2 tinned anchovy fillets, drained
and chopped

1 clove garlic

1 tablespoon salted capers, rinsed,
drained and roughly chopped

1 heaped tablespoon finely
chopped fresh basil

1 heaped tablespoon finely
chopped fresh parsley

1 teaspoon wholegrain mustard

3 tablespoons olive oil

1½ tablespoons lemon juice

1 heaped tablespoon finely
grated Parmesan

salt and freshly milled
black pepper

You will also need an ovenproof
baking dish, 7½ x 7½ x 1 inches
(19 x 19 x 2.5 cm), lightly buttered.

This recipe is delightfully different and makes a complete meal for two to three people with perhaps a simple green salad with a lemony dressing as an accompaniment. Skinless cod fillet is good in this, but any firm, thick white fish could be used – chunks of monkfish tail would be particularly good for a special occasion.

To begin this recipe, first crush the garlic with a teaspoon of salt, using a pestle and mortar, and, when it becomes a purée, simply add the anchovy fillets, capers and chopped basil and parsley, together with the mustard, 2 tablespoons olive oil, the lemon juice and some freshly milled black pepper, and whisk well to blend them thoroughly.

Now turn the oven on to gas mark 6, 400°F (200°C). Next, prepare the potatoes: put the kettle on, then peel and chop the potatoes into ¼ inch (5 mm) slices. Place them in a shallow saucepan, then add salt and just enough boiling water to barely cover them. Simmer, with a lid on, for 7-8 minutes – they need to be almost cooked but not quite – then drain off the water and cover them with a cloth for 2-3 minutes to absorb the steam.

Now arrange half the potatoes over the base of the baking dish and season well, wipe the fish with kitchen paper, cut it into 1½ inch (4 cm) chunks and scatter it on top of the potatoes, seasoning again. Next, spoon the purée all over and arrange the rest of the potato slices on top, overlapping them slightly. Then brush them lightly with the remaining tablespoon of olive oil, season once more and sprinkle the cheese over. Now bake the whole lot on a high shelf of the oven for about 30 minutes, by which time the fish will be cooked and the potatoes golden brown.

Escalopes of Veal in Marsala
Serves 2

2 veal escalopes (about 4 oz/110 g each); alternatively, use pork or turkey

6 fl oz (175 ml) Marsala

1 rounded tablespoon plain flour, seasoned with salt and freshly milled black pepper

2 dessertspoons olive oil

1 oz (25 g) butter

1 tablespoon balsamic vinegar

You will also need a large, 10 inch (25.5 cm) frying pan.

A simple classic that is quick and easy and never loses its charm. A good accompaniment would be cubes of potato tossed in oil and rosemary and baked crisp in a hot oven, along with a mixed-leaf green salad.

First, cut each veal escalope into 3 pieces, then lay them out on a chopping board with a large piece of clingfilm on top and gently beat the meat out, using a rolling pin. It needs to be about $\frac{1}{8}$–$\frac{1}{4}$ inch (3-5 mm) thick – but be fairly gentle with the rolling pin so as not to break the meat. When it is ready, coat each piece with seasoned flour, shaking off any excess.

Now, when you are ready to fry the veal, place the frying pan over a high heat and add the olive oil and butter to the pan. When the butter is foaming, add the escalope pieces and fry them on each side for 1½ minutes. When you have done this, add the Marsala and balsamic vinegar. Let this bubble away for about 3 minutes, or until the sauce is syrupy and glossy. Serve on warm plates with the sauce spooned over.

Ossobuco

Serves 4

4 large pieces shin of veal
(3 lb 4 oz/1.5 kg)

2 oz (50 g) butter

1 medium onion, roughly chopped

1 clove garlic, crushed

10 fl oz (275 ml) dry white wine

12 oz (350 g) ripe, red tomatoes

1 tablespoon tomato purée

salt and freshly milled
black pepper

For the gremolata

1 large clove garlic, finely chopped

2 heaped tablespoons chopped
fresh parsley

grated zest of 1 small lemon

You will also need a 6 pint
(3.5 litre) flameproof casserole,
with a tight-fitting lid, which can
hold the pieces of veal in one layer.

This is a famous Italian casserole: shin of veal cooked in white wine with tomatoes. Try to buy the pieces of shin about 2 inches (5 cm) thick. In Milan it is never cooked with tomatoes but simply braised in white wine and its own juices. You might like to try it minus tomatoes. Either way, it will be lovely.

First of all, skin the tomatoes by placing them in a heatproof bowl and pouring boiling water on to them. After exactly a minute, remove them from the water and slip off the skins, then chop the tomatoes into small pieces. Now in the casserole, melt 1 oz (25 g) of the butter and fry the onion and garlic till pale gold – about 10 minutes. Then remove them to a plate with a slotted spoon. Now add the rest of the butter and fry the pieces of veal, to brown them slightly on both sides. Then pour over the wine, and let it bubble and reduce a little before adding the onion, garlic, tomatoes, tomato purée and a seasoning of salt and freshly milled pepper.

Then cover the casserole and leave it to cook gently on the top of the stove for 1 hour. After that, take off the lid, and let it cook for another half an hour or so until the meat is tender and the sauce is reduced.

Before serving, to make the gremolata, mix the chopped garlic, parsley and lemon zest together, then sprinkle this all over the meat. Serve this with rice (preferably Risotto alla Milanese, see page 68), and don't forget to dig out the marrow from the centre of the bones – it's the best bit.

Veal Milanese
Serves 6

6 veal escalopes (about 3-4 oz/
75-110 g each); alternatively, use
pork or turkey

2 large eggs

2 rounded tablespoons flour
seasoned with salt and freshly
milled black pepper

8 oz (225 g) white breadcrumbs

2 oz (50 g) butter

2 tablespoons olive oil

2 lemons, quartered, to serve

salt and freshly milled
black pepper

You will also need a large, 10 inch
(25.5 cm) frying pan.

There is a little trattoria that Michael and I go to in Waterloo called La Barca and whenever I go, I always have this dish, served with a portion of Spaghetti with Ragù. I absolutely love this combination with the veal drenched in lemon juice. Otherwise, sautéed potatoes and a green salad which includes rocket would be good.

You need to start by making the veal escalopes a little thinner by beating the pieces of meat. So, place them between two large pieces of clingfilm and gently pound them, using a rolling pin, but be careful not to break the meat – it just needs to be stretched a little. Next, break the eggs into a shallow dish and lightly beat them together with some salt and freshly milled black pepper. Tip the breadcrumbs on to a large plate and put the seasoned flour on to another plate. Then dip each escalope, first into the flour, then the beaten egg and then into the breadcrumbs, shaking off the excess breadcrumbs as you go, and transferring the escalopes to another clean plate. Now heat half the butter and oil in the frying pan and, when sizzling hot, add 3 escalopes to the pan.

Cook them for 3-4 minutes on each side or till crisp and golden brown. Then drain on kitchen paper, and keep warm in a low oven while you cook the other escalopes in the rest of the butter and oil. Sprinkle with salt before serving with the lemons to squeeze over.

Beef in Barolo
with Parmesan Mashed Potatoes
Serves 6

2 lb 8 oz (1.15 kg) piece of braising
steak or brisket, rolled and tied

12 fl oz (340 ml) red wine,
made from the nebbiolo grape
or a barbera d'Alba or d'Asti,
(or Barolo if you're feeling flush)

2 dessertspoons olive oil

4 oz (110 g) carrot, peeled and
chopped

4 oz (110 g) celery, chopped

1 medium onion, chopped

2 cloves garlic

1 tablespoon chopped fresh
rosemary

2 bay leaves

salt and freshly milled
black pepper

For the potatoes

3 lb (1.35 kg) Desirée or King
Edward potatoes

8 fl oz (225 ml) hot milk

6 oz (175 g) grated Parmesan

salt and freshly milled
black pepper

You will also need a 4 pint
(2.25 litre), flameproof casserole.

This is a classic from Piedmont but because Barolo is such a very fine and quite expensive wine, I tend to make this with something less costly but from the same region. Then splash out and buy a bottle of Barolo to drink with it.

If you have time it's good to marinade the beef. Place it in a deep small pot that just fits it, then pour the wine over and leave it for 24 hours, turning it over once during the time.

To cook the beef, pre-heat the oven to gas mark 1, 275°F (140°C) and then heat 1 dessertspoon of the oil in a large, solid frying pan. Take the beef out of the marinade (reserve the wine) and dry the meat thoroughly with paper towels. Season it with salt and pepper and, when the oil is very hot, brown the beef on all sides, turning it around until it's browned. Then remove it to a plate, heat the rest of the oil and add the prepared vegetables and garlic to the pan and toss them around until they have turned brown at the edges.

Now place the beef and the vegetables in the casserole, pour in the reserved marinade and add the rosemary and the bay leaves. Then bring it up to simmering point, put a tight-fitting lid on, and transfer the casserole to the oven for 3 hours, turning the meat over at half time.

For the Parmesan mash, all you do is steam the potatoes, cut into even-sized pieces, for 20-25 minutes till tender. Then, with an electric hand whisk, beat in the milk and Parmesan cheese with a good seasoning of salt and pepper till the potatoes are light and fluffy.

To serve, remove the meat to a carving board, then remove and discard the bay leaves and whiz the vegetables and juices in a blender to make a smooth sauce. Taste to check the seasoning and serve the meat, cut in slices, with the sauce poured over. In Italy it is traditional to serve this with carrots.

Sea Bass with Salsa Verde
Serves 2

2 sea bass fillets (7-8 oz/200-225 g each) – sometimes farmed sea bass fillets are very small, in which case, use 2 per person (4½ oz/125 g each)

a little olive oil

½ lemon, quartered

salt and freshly milled black pepper

For the salsa verde

4 tinned anchovy fillets in oil, drained

1 tablespoon capers in vinegar, drained

1 teaspoon dry mustard powder

1 small clove garlic, crushed

1½ tablespoons lemon juice

6 tablespoons olive oil

2 tablespoons chopped fresh parsley

1 tablespoon chopped fresh basil

salt and freshly milled black pepper

This is an extremely fast supper dish for two people. Salsa verde is a strong-flavoured, quite gutsy sauce that does wonders for any grilled fish. It behaves rather like a very thick vinaigrette and, before serving, always needs to have another mix. Some small new potatoes would make a good accompaniment.

Begin by making the salsa verde. To start with, chop the anchovy fillets as small as possible and crush them to a paste in a mortar (if you haven't got a mortar, a small bowl and the end of a rolling pin will do). Put the capers in a small sieve and rinse them under cold, running water to remove the vinegar they were preserved in. Dry them on kitchen paper and chop them as minutely as you can and add them to the anchovies. Next, add the mustard, garlic, lemon juice and some freshly milled black pepper and mix well. Now add the oil and chopped herbs, mix again so that all the ingredients are properly combined and check the taste to see how much salt to add.

To cook the fish, you need to pre-heat the grill to its highest setting for at least 10 minutes. Next, line a grill tray with kitchen foil, brush the fish fillets on both sides with olive oil and place them on the tray, flesh side up. Season with salt and freshly milled black pepper, then grill for 5-6 minutes, turning halfway, or until just cooked through. Serve straightaway with the salsa verde and the lemon wedges to squeeze over.

Vitello Tonnato
Serves 8

2 lb 12 oz (1.25 kg) thick piece boneless veal topside

1 small onion, studded with a few cloves

2 bay leaves

2 celery stalks, halved

1 small carrot, peeled

6 black peppercorns

5 fl oz (150 ml) dry white wine

For the sauce

2 large eggs

1 fat clove garlic, peeled

10 fl oz (275 ml) groundnut or other flavourless oil

2 dessertspoons white wine vinegar

3 oz (75 g) best-quality tuna fish in a tin or jar, drained

2 tinned anchovy fillets, drained

1½ tablespoons salted capers, rinsed and drained

1 tablespoon lemon juice (or more, to taste)

salt and freshly milled black pepper

To garnish

a few extra capers

2 tinned anchovy fillets, drained and very thinly sliced

½ lemon, sliced

Pre-heat the oven to gas mark 4, 350°F (180°C).

This famous Italian classic is served cold. It's perfect in summer for a buffet, served with tiny new potatoes and a lemony, green salad.

Begin by putting the veal in a medium roasting tin with the onion, bay leaves, celery stalks, carrot, peppercorns and wine. Then, roast the veal in the pre-heated oven for 1¼ hours.

For the sauce, you need to start by making a mayonnaise. So, break the whole eggs straight into the goblet of a blender or food processor, add the garlic clove and 1 teaspoon salt. Then measure the oil into a jug and switch the machine on. To blend everything thoroughly, pour the oil in a thin, very steady trickle with the motor running. You must be very careful here – too much oil in too soon means the sauce will curdle. When all the oil is in, add the white wine vinegar and blend. Then add the tuna, anchovy fillets and capers and whiz again till smooth. Now do a bit of tasting and season with lemon juice and pepper. The sauce can be made well ahead and kept in the fridge till needed.

When the veal is ready, take it out of the oven and leave everything to get cold. After that, take the veal out of the tin – you can discard the vegetables, bay leaves, peppercorns and any remaining wine now. Slice the meat very thinly and arrange it in a large, shallow serving dish. Spoon the sauce over the meat. Now arrange the anchovy slices in a zig-zag pattern on top. Scatter over a few extra capers and garnish with the lemon slices.

Liver Veneziana
Serves 2

8 oz (225 g) calves' liver

2 medium onions, halved
and thinly sliced, and the layers
separated into half-moon shapes

10 fl oz (275 ml) white wine,
such as a dry Soave

2 tablespoons olive oil

1 large clove garlic, crushed

½ oz (10 g) butter

salt and freshly milled
black pepper

You will also need 2 medium
frying pans.

This is the famous classic from Venice (or rather my version). While Soave is the traditional wine of the region, I sometimes make a version using Marsala, which is also extremely good.

In the first frying pan, heat 1 tablespoon of the oil, then add the onions and, keeping the heat fairly high, toss them around to brown to a dark – almost black – colour round the edges. Then add the garlic and toss that round before pouring in the wine. Add some seasoning and bring everything up to simmering point, then turn the heat down to its lowest setting and let it just barely bubble, without covering, for 45 minutes.

Meanwhile, prepare the liver, slicing it into the thinnest possible strips, approximately 1½ inches (4 cm) in length. It is most important to keep them thin to cook as quickly as possible. When the 45 minutes are up, heat the remaining tablespoon of oil, along with the butter, in the other frying pan and, when the butter foams, add the strips of liver and sear them very briefly. Toss them around for only 1-2 minutes to brown at the edges – be swift and careful, as overcooking will dry them too much. Season the liver with salt and freshly milled black pepper. Then remove the pan from the heat, add the onions from the other pan, mix together, and serve immediately.

Sfogi in Saor
Serves 4-6

1 lb (450 g) skinless sole fillets or plaice fillets

1 oz (25 g) plain flour

4 fl oz (120 ml) olive oil

2 tablespoons sultanas

1 large onion, thinly sliced

3 fl oz (75 ml) good-quality red wine vinegar

4 fl oz (120 ml) dry white wine

2 small cinnamon sticks

2 tablespoons pine nuts

pared rind of a small orange, cut into strips

4 bay leaves

salt and freshly milled black pepper

This is a classic Venetian dish which has been given to me by our Editor, Sarah Randell. *Sfogi* (sole) is pronounced 'sforgey'. It is a lovely sweet and sour combination.

First of all, season the flour and lightly dust the fish fillets with it, tapping off the excess as you go. Then heat 3 tablespoons of the oil in a large, non-stick frying pan and when it is sizzling, fry the fish on both sides (2-3 minutes on each) in batches until lightly golden and crisp. Remove the cooked fillets to a plate lined with kitchen paper. Now arrange the fish in a single layer in a serving dish and wipe out the frying pan.

Now put the sultanas in a small bowl, cover them with warm water and leave them to soak and plump up. Then heat 2 more tablespoons of olive oil in the pan and stir in the thinly sliced onion. Reduce the temperature to low, cover with a lid, and leave the onions to gently stew for 20-25 minutes until soft and translucent, stirring occasionally. When the time is up, increase the heat and add the vinegar, wine and cinnamon sticks to the pan. Boil the mixture, uncovered, for 3 minutes and then take the pan off the heat. Now, drain the sultanas and stir them into the onions with the remaining 3 tablespoons of olive oil, the pine nuts and pared orange rind and season with salt and freshly milled black pepper.

Finally, pour the marinade over the fish and tuck the bay leaves among the fillets. Now leave everything to cool, then cover and refrigerate for 24 hours before using. Serve the fish at room temperature with good Italian bread.

Puddings

Puddings Puddings

Zabaglione
Serves 4

4 large egg yolks

1 tablespoon light muscovado sugar

1 teaspoon cornflour

5 fl oz (150 ml) Marsala

I have to admit that the classic way of making this is in a bowl fitted over barely simmering water – which does take 20 minutes' whisking; so for busy people like us, adding a teaspoon of cornflour means you can whisk it over direct heat without it splitting and you won't know the cornflour is there.

Begin by putting the egg yolks in a medium bowl and then add the sugar and the cornflour. Now, using an electric hand whisk (or hand whisk if you are feeling energetic), whisk everything together until light and fluffy – about 3 minutes – then pour in the Marsala, a little at a time, and keep whisking until smooth.

Next, pour this mixture into a medium saucepan and put over a low to medium heat. Keep whisking the mixture all the time until it thickens, which will take about 5-10 minutes (depending on whether you use an electric or hand whisk). When it has thickened, it should be light and foamy. It is best served warm fairly soon after making, and is divine with a fruit compote.

Tiramisù
Serves 6

3 large egg yolks, plus 2 large egg whites

2 oz (50 g) golden caster sugar

9 oz (250 g) mascarpone

5 oz (150 g) sponge fingers or boudoir biscuits (about 24)

5 fl oz (150 ml) very strong espresso coffee

3 tablespoons dark rum

2 oz (50 g) dark chocolate (70-75 per cent cocoa solids), chopped

1 tablespoon cocoa powder

You will also need 6 stemmed glasses, each with a capacity of 7 fl oz (200 ml).

There isn't a classic recipe for tiramisù as such, as there are many varying versions both in Italy and around the world, but the following one is, I think, the nicest I've come across. For lovers of strong coffee, dark chocolate and the rich creaminess of mascarpone it is one of the nicest, easiest and most popular desserts.

First, put the egg yolks into a medium bowl, together with the sugar, and beat with an electric hand whisk on high speed for about 3 minutes, or until the mixture forms a light, pale mousse. In a separate, large, grease-free bowl, stir the mascarpone with a wooden spoon to soften it, then gradually beat in the egg yolk mixture. Between each addition, beat well until the mixture is smooth before adding more. Now wash and dry the beaters of the whisk so they are perfectly clean, then in a third separate, grease-free bowl, whisk the egg whites until they form soft peaks. Now lightly fold this into the mascarpone mixture and then put the bowl to one side.

Next, break the biscuits in half, then pour the coffee and rum into a shallow dish and then dip the sponge fingers briefly into it, turning them over – they will absorb the liquid very quickly. Now simply layer the desserts by putting 3 of the soaked sponge halves into each glass, followed by a tablespoon of mascarpone mixture and a layer of chopped chocolate. Repeat the whole process, putting 5 halves in next, followed by the mascarpone, finishing with a layer of chopped chocolate and a final dusting of cocoa powder. Cover the glasses with clingfilm, then chill in the fridge for several hours and serve straight from the fridge – I think it tastes better very cold.

Note This recipe contains raw eggs.

Peaches Baked with Amaretti
Serves 4

4 large, ripe but firm, peaches

2 oz (50 g) Amaretti biscuits, crushed

2 dessertspoons golden caster sugar

1 large egg yolk

1 oz (25 g) butter, softened

To serve

a little icing sugar

chilled pouring cream or mascarpone

You will also need an ovenproof baking dish, 6 x 9 inches (15 x 23 cm).

Pre-heat the oven to gas mark 4, 350°F (180°C).

This is a recipe I have adapted from one of my most favourite cookbooks, the *Four Seasons Cookery Book,* by Margaret Costa (Grub Street Publishing).

Begin by halving the peaches and removing their stones. Now mix together the sugar, egg yolk, butter and the crushed Amaretti. Give everything a good stir, then spoon the filling into the peach halves. Pile it up to use it all.

Now put the peach halves in the ovenproof dish and place it on the centre shelf of the oven. Bake, without covering, for about 30 minutes. Then remove the peaches from the oven, dust with icing sugar, and serve hot with chilled pouring cream or mascarpone.

Cassata Siciliana
Serves 6-8

10 fl oz (275 ml) Marsala

grated zest and juice of 1 orange

7 oz (200 g) mango and cranberry fruit mix (raisins, golden sultanas, dried mango and cranberry) or other mixed dried fruit

1 lb 2 oz (500 g) ricotta

5 oz (150 g) mascarpone

2 oz (50 g) chocolate drops

1 oz (25 g) natural pistachio nuts, roughly chopped

3 oz (75 g) golden caster sugar

6 oz (175 g) sponge fingers or boudoir biscuits (about 30)

You will also need a 2 lb (900 g) loaf tin (3 x 8 x 2½ inches/ 7.5 x 20 x 6 cm).

This delightful Italian dessert is really just an assembly job as far as you're concerned, but everyone will think you're very clever!

Begin by pouring the Marsala and orange juice into a small saucepan and heating gently. Then add the dried fruits, and remove the pan from the heat to allow them to steep in the liquid for half an hour until they have swelled slightly. Then drain them in a sieve set over a bowl to catch the liquid and leave to get cold.

Meanwhile, in a large bowl, mix together the ricotta and mascarpone, then add the chocolate drops, orange zest, chopped pistachios and sugar, give everything a good stir, then mix in the drained fruit when it is cold. Now line the base and long sides of the loaf tin with the sponge fingers, dipped first in the reserved Marsala and orange juice and trimmed to fit comfortably. They need to be put in sugar side down. Reserve 8 soaked sponge fingers for the top. After that, any remaining liquid can be sprinkled over the biscuits in the tin. Next, spoon in the ricotta and fruit mixture, patting it down into the tin to remove any air bubbles. Finally, place the remaining soaked biscuits on top. Cover tightly with clingfilm and refrigerate overnight. Next day, serve cut into thin slices – it doesn't need any accompaniment as it's really yummy as it is.

Harry's Bar Torta di Zabaglione
Serves 8-10

For the zabaglione filling

3 large egg yolks

3 oz (75 g) golden caster sugar

1½ oz (40 g) plain flour, sifted

9 fl oz (250 ml) Marsala

12 fl oz (340 ml) double cream

For the cake

4 oz (110 g) self-raising flour

½ teaspoon baking powder

2 large eggs, at room temperature

4 oz (110 g) very soft butter

4 oz (110 g) golden caster sugar

¼ teaspoon pure vanilla extract

a little sifted icing sugar, to dust

You will also need a sponge tin, 8 x 8 x 1½ inches (20 x 20 x 4 cm), lightly greased, and the base lined with baking parchment.

This is a truly wonderful cake, which I first ate in Harry's Dolci, my favourite Venetian restaurant. The original recipe is printed in *The Harry's Bar Cookbook* by Arrigo Cipriani (Blake Publishing).

First of all, make the zabaglione filling. Using an electric hand whisk, beat the egg yolks for 1 minute in a medium bowl, then add the sugar and beat until the mixture is thick and pale yellow (this takes about 3 minutes). Next, whisk in the flour a tablespoon at a time, mixing in very thoroughly, then gradually whisk in the Marsala.

Now tip the mixture into a medium, heavy-based saucepan and place over a medium heat. Then, cook the mixture, stirring constantly, until it has thickened and is just about to boil; this will take about 5 minutes. Don't worry if it looks a bit lumpy, just tip it into a clean bowl, then whisk until smooth again. Let the custard cool, whisking it from time to time to stop a skin forming. When it is cold, cover with clingfilm and pop in the fridge for at least 2 hours. Pre-heat the oven to gas mark 3, 325°F (170°C).

Meanwhile, make the cake. To do this, take a large mixing bowl, place the flour and baking powder in a sieve and sift into the bowl, holding the sieve high to give them a good airing as they go down. Now all you do is simply add the other cake ingredients, except the icing sugar, to the bowl and, provided the butter is really soft, just go in with the electric hand whisk and whisk everything together until you have a smooth, well combined mixture, which will take about 1 minute. What you will now end up with is a mixture that drops off a spoon when you give it a tap on the side of the bowl. If it seems a bit stiff, add a little water and mix again.

Now spoon the mixture into the tin, level it out with the back of a spoon and place the tin on the centre shelf of the oven. The cake will take 30-35 minutes to cook, but don't open the oven door until 30 minutes have elapsed. To test whether it is cooked or not, touch the centre lightly with a finger: if it leaves no impression and the sponge springs back, it is ready. Remove it from the oven, then wait about 5 minutes before turning it out on to a wire cooling rack. Carefully peel off the base paper, which is easier if you make a fold in the paper first, then pull it gently away without trying to lift it off. Now leave the sponge to cool completely.

To assemble the torta, whip the double cream in a large bowl until stiff, then add the zabaglione custard to the bowl and whisk again until thoroughly mixed. Place the cake flat on a board, then, holding a serrated palette knife horizontally, carefully slice it into 2 thin halves. Next, reserve 2-3 heaped tablespoons of the zabaglione filling to decorate the sides of the cake and spread the rest of the filling over the bottom half, easing it gently to the edges. Place the other cake half on top and press down very gently. Before you spread the mixture on the sides of the cake, it's a good idea to brush away any loose crumbs, so they don't get mixed up in it. Now, using a small palette knife, spread the reserved filling evenly all around the sides of the cake. Finally, dust the top with the icing sugar before serving. If the cake is made and decorated ahead of time, store it, covered, in the fridge to keep it firm, but remove it half an hour before serving.

Torta di Mele
Serves 6-8

For the pastry

12 oz (350 g) self-raising flour, plus a little extra for rolling out

6 oz (175 g) cold butter, cubed

2 tablespoons golden caster sugar

zest of ½ lemon

1 teaspoon ground cinnamon

2 large eggs, lightly beaten

For the filling

2 lb (900 g) apples (I like to use ½ Cox's apples and ½ Bramleys)

1 tablespoon lemon juice, for the apples

2 tablespoons golden caster sugar

1 teaspoon ground cinnamon

zest of ½ lemon

a little milk for brushing the top

icing sugar for dusting

You will also need an 8 x 2¼ inches (20 x 5.5 cm) deep, loose-bottomed, springform tin, very lightly buttered.

This is a famous Italian apple dessert, which is sometimes spongy like a cake, and sometimes crisper, more like pastry – mine is the latter.

For the pastry, sift the flour, then place it in a processor with the cubed butter, sugar, lemon zest and cinnamon, then switch it on and process to the fine crumb stage. Then add the eggs and process again till you have a stiff dough. Remove it from the processor, wrap in clingfilm and leave it to rest in the fridge for 30 minutes.

Meanwhile, pre-heat the oven to gas mark 6, 400°F (200°C) and prepare the apples by peeling and cutting them into ½ inch (1 cm) slices, keeping them in cold water to which a tablespoon of lemon juice has been added, to prevent them browning. Then cut off a third of the pastry and, on a very generously floured board, roll out the large piece to line the inside of the tin. It will be fragile and break easily but honestly, all you need to do is simply squeeze the pastry across the base and sides of the tin, repairing any cracks as you go.

Next, drain the apples, patting them dry with a clean tea towel. Fill the pastry case with the apples, sprinkling in the sugar, cinnamon and lemon zest as you go. Then finally, roll out the reserved third of the pastry for the top and position it over the apples, sealing round the edges with your fingers and squeezing together any cracks. Brush the surface with milk, make steam holes in the centre, and bake on the centre shelf of the oven for 45-50 minutes or until a skewer inserted tells you the apples are cooked. Cool for about 20 minutes before unmoulding and serve, dusted with icing sugar. This is great with pouring cream, or for sheer indulgence, how about some mascarpone?

Coffee Granita
Serves 4

1 pint (570 ml) strong espresso coffee (made in an espresso coffee maker) or extremely strong filter coffee (the dark Continental roast is best)

4 oz (110 g) golden granulated sugar

whipped cream, to serve

You will also need a shallow, 1½ pint (850 ml) plastic freezer container.

This recipe was given to me by one of my favourite chefs and food writers, Simon Hopkinson. It's so simple, refreshing and very attractive served in glasses with lots of whipped cream.

Begin by dissolving the sugar in the hot coffee. Allow it to cool, then pour it into the container and place it in the freezer. As soon as it has begun to form ice crystals around the edge, stir it with a fork to distribute the ice. (In a conventional freezer it can take 2-3 hours to reach this stage – so keep an eye on it.) After that, keep returning and forking the ice crystals around until you have no liquid coffee left. This can take up to another 3 hours, but it is impossible to be exact, as freezers vary.

You can serve the coffee granita at this point. Or, if you are making it ahead, all you do is remove it from the freezer to the main body of the fridge 20 minutes before serving. To break up the ice, use a strong fork: this is not meant to be like a sorbet, but is served as coffee-flavoured ice crystals. Topped with whipped cream, it is a lovely, refreshing way to end a good meal.

Pear Charlotte
Serves 6

1 lb 12 oz (800 g) ripe but firm pears

1½ lemons, unwaxed are best for this recipe if you can find them

5 fl oz (150 ml) dry white wine

5 oz (150 g) golden caster sugar, plus a little extra, if required

1 teaspoon ground cinnamon

1 teaspoon ground cloves

4½ oz (125 g) sponge fingers or boudoir biscuits (about 21)

2 tablespoons Poire William eau-de-vie, Grappa or Calvados

crème fraîche, to serve

You will also need a large frying pan with a lid, and a 2 pint (1.2 litre) pudding basin, lined with clingfilm.

A simple interpretation of an old classic, this elegant recipe from Anna Del Conte hails from Northern Italy. Anna served this to us and we loved it so much she has given me her own recipe for this book. It's also very good made with apples.

First of all, wash and dry the lemons. Then, using a potato peeler, peel off 3 strips of zest from one and set aside. Squeeze the lemons and pour the juice into a bowl.

Now peel the pears, quarter and core them and slice very thinly. Put these slices into the bowl and mix so they are coated with lemon juice. This will prevent the pears from discolouring as well as giving them a lovely flavour. Leave them to macerate for an hour.

Next, put the wine and 5 fl oz (150 ml) water in the large frying pan, then add the sugar, spices and lemon strips and put over a low heat until the sugar has dissolved, stirring constantly. Simmer gently for 5 minutes and then slide in the pears and their juices. Turn them over a few times for the first 2-3 minutes or so, then cover and cook over a very low heat until they are tender. This will take only a few minutes if you have sliced them thinly. Taste and add a little more sugar, if necessary. It is difficult to give an exact amount, as it depends on the quality of the pears.

Lift the pears out of the pan with a slotted spoon and set them aside, then discard the lemon peel. Turn the heat up and reduce the juices until they are heavy with syrup and rich with flavour. Mix in the liqueur.

Soak the biscuits in the syrup just enough to soften them, then line the basin with them. Spoon the pears into the basin and cover with more soaked biscuits. Finally, pour over 3 tablespoons of remaining syrup, cover with clingfilm and chill for 6 hours.

To unmould the charlotte, remove the clingfilm from the top and place a round plate over the basin. Turn the plate and basin the other way up, lift the basin off and peel off the clingfilm lining. Serve with a bowl of crème fraîche.

How To Cook Perfect Pasta

Always use a very large cooking pot, making sure you have at least 4 pints (2.25 litres) of water to every 8 oz (225 g) of pasta, with 1 level tablespoon of salt added. I recommend this quantity of dried pasta for spaghetti or any other shape if being served with just sauce. This will serve two as a main course, or use 4-6 oz (110-175 g) as a starter. Before the pasta goes in, make sure the water is up to a good fierce boil. Add the pasta as quickly as possible and stir it around just once to separate it. If you're cooking long pasta such as spaghetti, push it against the base of the pan and, as you feel it give, keep pushing until it all collapses down into the water.

You don't need to put a lid on the pan: if it's really boiling briskly it will come back to the boil in seconds and, if you put a lid on, it will boil over. Put a timer on and give it 10-12 minutes for top-quality pasta, but because this timing varies according to the shape and quality of the pasta, the only real way to tell is to taste it. So do this after 8 minutes, then 9, and 10, and so on. This only applies when you cook a particular brand for the first time. After that, you will always know how long it takes. Sometimes you can give it 1 minute's less boiling and then allow an extra minute's cooking while you combine it with the sauce.

Have a colander ready in the sink, then, as you are draining the water, swirl it around the colander, which will heat it ready for the hot pasta. Don't drain it too thoroughly: it's good to have a few drops of moisture still clinging, as this prevents the pasta from becoming dry. Place the colander containing the pasta back over the saucepan to catch any drips.

Always serve the pasta on deep, warmed plates or bowls to keep it as hot as possible as it goes to the table. For spaghetti, the very best way to serve it is to use pasta tongs, and always lift it high to quickly separate each portion from the rest.

Presto pronto! – in Italian this means soon and quickly. Always work quickly, as pasta won't hang around – if it cools it goes sticky and gluey, so drain it quickly, serve it quickly and eat it quickly.

If the pasta is going to be cooked again, in a baked dish such as macaroni cheese, for example, give it half the usual cooking time to allow for the time in the oven.

Mini Focaccia Bread
Makes 4 mini or 1 large focaccia

Focaccia is an Italian flat bread made with olive oil. What's good about it is that it gives you scope to invent all kinds of interesting toppings and you can vary them as you like. Arrange your chosen topping over (or into) the whole thing.

12 oz (350 g) plain white flour, plus extra for dusting

½ teaspoon salt

2 teaspoons easy-blend dried yeast

7½ fl oz (210 ml) warm water

2½ tablespoons extra virgin olive oil

4 teaspoons crushed sea salt

Begin by sifting the flour and salt into a large mixing bowl, then sprinkle in the yeast and mix that in. Next pour in the warm water, along with 1½ tablespoons of the olive oil, and mix everything to a dough that leaves the sides of the bowl clean (if necessary, add a few more drops of warm water).

Now turn the dough out on to a lightly floured surface and knead it for 10 minutes (or you can use an electric mixer with a dough hook and process for 5 minutes).

When the dough feels very bouncy and elastic, return it to the bowl, cover with clingfilm and leave in a warm place until it has doubled in size (about 1½ hours or more depending on the heat in the kitchen: if there's no suitable warm place, you can sit the bowl over a saucepan of warm water – but not over direct heat).

After that, turn the dough out on to the work surface and punch the air out by kneading it again for 2-3 minutes. Now, divide the dough into 4, put the pieces on an oiled baking sheet and use your hands to pull and push each one into a sort of oblong, rounded at the ends and measuring 3 x 4 inches (7.5 x 10 cm).

Then drizzle the rest of the olive oil over the surface of each one and sprinkle the sea salt over. Cover with a damp tea towel and leave for 30 minutes for the dough to puff up.

Meanwhile, pre-heat the oven to gas mark 5, 375°F (190°C). Bake the focaccias for about 15 minutes or until they are golden round the edges and look well cooked in the centre. Transfer them to a wire rack to cool a little and serve warm.

If you're making a full-sized focaccia, pat the dough out into an oval shape 12 x 10 inches (30 x 25.5 cm) – it will take 25-30 minutes to cook.

Conversions for Australia and New Zealand

Measurements in this book refer to British standard imperial and metric measurements.

The standard UK teaspoon measure is 5 ml, the dessertspoon is 10 ml and the tablespoon measure is 15 ml. In Australia, the standard tablespoon is 20 ml.

UK large eggs weigh 63-73 g.

Converting standard cups to imperial and metric weights

Ingredients (1 cup)	Imperial/metric
basil, fresh, whole*	2 oz/50 g
butter	9 oz/250 g
cabbage, shredded	3 oz/75 g
cannellini beans	7 oz/200 g
carrot, finely chopped	5 oz/150 g
chocolate, chopped	5 oz/150 g
dried fruit, mixed	4½ oz/125 g
fontina, small cubes	5 oz/150 g
flour, plain/self-raising	4½ oz/125 g
mascarpone cheese	8 oz/225 g
mozzarella, grated	5 oz/150 g
mushrooms, small, sliced	3½ oz/95 g
olives, pitted	4½ oz/125 g
onion, chopped	5 oz/150 g
pancetta, chopped	5 oz/150 g
Parmesan, finely grated	4 oz/110 g
parsley, flat leaf, whole	¾ oz/20 g
pecorino, grated*	3½ oz/95 g
penne or similar, uncooked	3½ oz/95 g
pine nuts	5 oz/150 g
pistachio, nuts, chopped	4½ oz/125 g
rice, risotto, uncooked	8 oz/225 g
ricotta cheese	9 oz/250 g
rocket leaves, whole*	1½ oz/40 g
semolina	4½ oz/125 g
spinach, raw, baby English*	2 oz/50 g
sugar, caster/golden caster	9 oz/250 g
tomatoes, fresh, chopped	7 oz/200 g
tomatoes, tinned, chopped	9 oz/250 g
walnuts, chopped	4½ oz/125 g

*Firmly packed

Liquid cup conversions

Imperial	Metric	Cups
1 fl oz	25 ml	⅛ cup
2 fl oz	55 ml	¼ cup
2¾ fl oz	70 ml	⅓ cup
4 fl oz	120 ml	½ cup
6 fl oz	175 ml	¾ cup
8 fl oz	225 ml	1 cup
10 fl oz	275 ml	1¼ cups
12 fl oz	340 ml	1½ cups
16 fl oz	450 ml	2 cups
1 pint	570 ml	2½ cups
24 fl oz	680 ml	3 cups
32 fl oz	1 litre	4 cups

A few ingredient names

aubergine
eggplant

Bramley apples
use green cooking apples

chocolate drops
chocolate melts

courgettes
zucchini

Cox's apples
use small dessert apples

Desirée potatoes
use other waxy, fleshed potatoes

double/whipping cream
use thick cream

golden caster/granulated sugar
use caster/granulated sugar

King Edward potatoes
use other floury potatoes

pepper, red/yellow/green
capsicum

sea bass
use snapper, hapuku or jewfish

shallots
eschalots/French shallots

spinach
use English spinach

spring onions
salad onion/shallots

tomato purée
tomato paste

Index

Delia Smith is Britain's best-selling cookery author, whose books have sold over 16 million copies.

Delia's other books include *How To Cook Books One, Two* and *Three, The Delia Collection: Soup, Chicken, Pork, Fish* and *Chocolate,* her *Vegetarian Collection,* the *Complete Illustrated Cookery Course, One Is Fun,* the *Summer* and *Winter Collections* and *Christmas.* She has launched her own website. Delia is also a director of Norwich City Football Club, where she is in charge of Canary Catering, several restaurants and a regular series of food and wine workshops.

She is married to the writer and editor Michael Wynn Jones and they live in Suffolk.

For more information on Delia's restaurant,
food and wine workshops and events, contact:
Delia's Canary Catering, Norwich City Football Club, Carrow Road,
Norwich NR1 1JE; www.deliascanarycatering.co.uk
For Delia's Canary Catering (conferencing and events enquiries),
telephone 01603 218704
For Delia's Restaurant and Bar (reservations),
telephone 01603 218705

Visit Delia's website at www.deliaonline.com